Administering

the Individualized Instruction

Program

Administering
the Individualized Instruction
Program

James Lewis, Jr.

Parker Publishing Company, Inc.

West Nyack, New York

Library of Congress
Catalog Card Number: 78-122320

PRINTED IN THE UNITED STATES OF AMERICA
ISBN-0-13-005199-3
B&P

To my mother

*who has endured more than the
usual amount of suffering.*

The new revolutionaries of education must soothe those who fear delight. Many a liberal educational reform has foundered on lack of specific tools for accomplishing its purposes—even if a tool may be something as simple as knowing precisely when to leave the learner entirely alone. Education must use its most powerful servant, technique, in teaching skills that go far beyond those which submit to academic achievement tests. Even today, as will be seen, specific, systematic ways are being worked out to help people learn to love, to feel deeply, to expand their inner selves, to create, to enter new realms of being.

George B. Leonard

By the same author:

A CONTEMPORARY APPROACH TO NONGRADED EDUCATION

Establishing the Basis
for Individualized Instruction

I have been asked by educators for the "secret" of my determination to produce an instrument for the individualization of instruction. My answer has always been that I still remember what it was to be turned off by a textbook which was utterly foreign because it bore no relation to those realities which constituted my existence as a poor child who belonged to an ethnic minority confined to a ghetto.

I have gone on to describe the particular atmosphere of the ghetto in which I grew up and the kinds of public schools which I attended and which tended to miseducate me and many of my fellow students. The miseducation was, perhaps, the lesser of the evils. By far the greater evils were the poor self-image and limited life-goal concept, which eventually led to an empty life for some of my schoolmates and no life at all for others. As an educator, my primary goals have been and must always be colored by my vivid recall of those school days. Originally, I knew that I had to provide an educational "banquet" which was more meaningful and more appetizing for children who came to school expecting nothing and too often left school without having received anything of lasting value to them.

I searched the nation's schools, looking, listening, and talking with noted experts about longstanding educational problems and equally longstanding educational philosophies. Nor were these visitations enough. In my spare hours, to the despair of my family, I pored over innumerable articles, texts and polemics pertaining to "progressive education," "quality education," "compensatory education" and "more effective education." Then I remember a particularly gray day when I sat pondering the problems inherent in a nongraded concept of education and made a list of those it would be necessary to eliminate if an effective individualized program of instruction were ever to be implemented. From this, I devised a tentative individualized program, skirting these "educational hazards" and concentrating on the kind of instructional programs that facilitate real learning on the part of the student and inspired teaching on the part of the teacher. In connection with my interest in this subject, I was fortunate to have had an opportunity to attend the First Annual Conference of a new organization which calls itself Individualizing Teaching and Learning: Worldwide Association. At this Conference I came in contact with other educators concerned with the same problems, whose comments and criticisms helped immeasurably in terms of crystallizing my own thinking—the thinking which finally resulted in the production of an individual study unit as an instrument which would bring relevance to the educational process, placing meaningfulness in the forefront of a humane and effective method to encourage learning with greater success than ever before in the past.

For years, teachers have noticed the differences in individual students. They have observed these differences in students' physical abilities, mental abilities, talents and interest. They have even observed these differences in the varied ways in which students move through the educational program. Yet, upon observing the average classroom milieu, one will invariably see the teacher standing in front of some thirty

11

students, "communicating" to all, as though all students learn at the same rate and are interested in the same subject matter. Occasionally, in order to make some allowances for individual differences, the teacher will divide the class into two or three groups. The only difference is that he now teaches three groups instead of one. An alternate technique used by some schools to individualize the instructional program is the use of multiple texts, but this, too, has limited effectiveness. Educators have continued to experiment with new methods and techniques to meet the varied needs of each student. Special grouping patterns were tried, such as tracking, phasing, ability grouping, and the Joplin Plan. These individual grouping techniques did very little to individualize the instructional program. In fact, in certain cases, homogeneous grouping was found harmful to some students. The increased emphasis given to educational technology made many educators feel that mechanization was surely a method to accommodate the individual differences among youngsters. These attempts were only partial attempts to bring about an individualized instructional program. The surest way to attend to the individual needs of students has always been simply to spend time with each student singly; however, exorbitant costs and lack of manpower usually forbade such special attentions.

A school devoted to individualized instruction must be oriented to allow each child to move at his own pace, through a learning program custom-tailored to meet his own unique interests, needs and abilities. This individualized learning program would provide for differences in entering levels of ability; differences in rate of learning to achieve the curricular, behavioral and attitudinal objectives; and even differences in the learning goals themselves. Such a program would have to place more responsibility for learning on the student, where it should have been concentrated in the first place. By providing learning experiences and learning activity options reinforced by a continuous process of self-assessment, the student would be encouraged to become a self-directed and self-initiating learner as he progresses through the educational program.

The standardized textbook does not afford the teacher or the student with the flexibility necessary in order to effectively individualize the instructional program. Therefore, any school district seeking to meet the varied needs of its students through an individualized approach in education must use an educational instrument which has been devised to provide this flexibility. The nongraded concept is being implemented in all of the schools which utilize this instrument for the individualization of instruction. Westinghouse Corporation, in collaboration with several schools throughout the country, utilizes the Teaching Learning Unit (TLU) as an educational instrument for their Computer-Assisted Instruction project. The Temple City School District in Temple City, California, while implementing differentiated staffing, has also introduced an instrument to facilitate the individualization of instruction. In addition to this, they have also initiated modular and flexible scheduling with a team teaching approach which is enhanced by the differentiated staffing technique. Both the United States Air Force and the Duluth, Minnesota, Public Schools utilize the Contract method which has been introduced as a means for individualizing the instructional program. A nongraded school district with flexible scheduling which has been cited for innovative practices, the Ruby L. Thomas Elementary School in Las Vegas, Nevada, has introduced the Individual Student Unit. The renowned Nova School District in Fort Lauderdale, Florida, which has implemented the nongraded concept, has introduced the famous Learning Activity Packages (LAP). The Wyandanch Public Schools of Wyandanch, Long Island, New York, in its nongraded elementary setting has created the Individual Study Unit (ISU). A private foundation, The Kettering Institute, supports the IDEA Materials Center in Laguna, California, which contracted with noted educational experts who came up with an instrument called the Unipac, presently in use by more than 50,000 children in more than 2,400 school districts throughout the country. The University of Pittsburgh, in collaboration with Research for Better Schools, has developed Individually Prescribed Instruction (IPI), which is being implemented by a number of school districts across the country.

An Individual Study Unit can be described as a learning kit, a teaching device, a learning package or an educational instrument, the purpose of which is to facilitate a change in learning behavior based upon an agreement between a student and his teacher. This change is to be produced in a systematic manner which will provide optimum opportunities for success in learning independently in small, medium and large group settings. This contemporary instructional student-teacher guide is a systematic managerial technique for developing, planning, implementing and evaluating the instructional program.

Figure A analyzes the path of a student through the individualized learning program using the Individual Study Unit concept. It illustrates the basic components of the Individual Study Unit, the order in which major tasks are undertaken, and the learning experiences and options available to the students and teachers.

The student initiates his program when he becomes intellectually aroused and stimulated by reading a statement of the purpose for progressing through the unit. If learning is to be self-initiated, the student must understand *what* materials are to be studied and *why* they should be studied. The student next receives a statement of the specific objectives of the unit. These objectives are well-delineated in terms of detailed and specific statements of the expected outcomes of the learning program insofar as these are demonstrated by observable competence and performance. An effective instrument for individualizing the instructional program must provide the student with a clear statement of what he is to accomplish through the learning program, and must encourage him to accept full responsibility for his learning. The Pre-Test is administered before the learner progresses through the unit to determine if he should continue in this unit or receive another unit to continue his learning. Planning and developing an instructional program which is truly individualized requires an exact diagnosis of the present level of the student. The left arrows in Figure A indicate that if the student passes the Pre-Test at a certain minimum standard, he may proceed to the attitudinal objectives or the evaluative section of the learning program. Self-Assessment is also an important component of IS Units to enable the student to check his progress. The Pre-Test can be used for the Self-Test. If a Self-Assessment Test is supplied with the unit, it is usually presented after the Learning Experience.

The nucleus of the learning program in IS Units is embraced by the Learning Experience and the Learning Activity Options. In this section, provision is made for individual entrance levels, motivations, abilities, talents, interest and learning style. The Learning Experience activates the thought process and introduces relevancy into the program. In order to give the student a voice in *how* he is going to learn, various options are listed for student selection. After the student completes the Learning

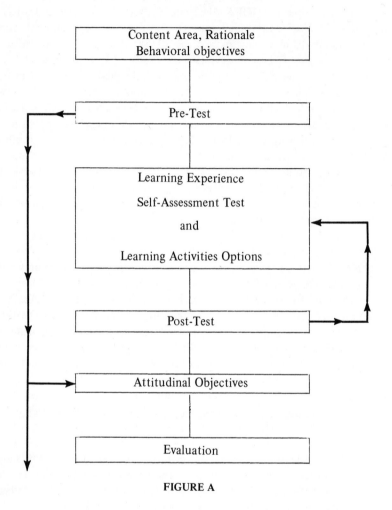

FIGURE A

Sequential Development of IS Units
Schematic

Note that the left arrows indicate that if the student passes the Pre-Test, he may proceed to the section of Attitudinal Objectives for a determination of his attitudes about the particular unit under study or he may be directed to another unit. The right arrows indicate that if the student is unsuccessful with the Post-Test he is recycled to the Learning Experience and Learning Activities Options where he or the teacher will select additional options to further the student's learning experience.

Experience and Options, a Post-Test is administered to the student to determine if a number of correct responses have been maintained by his unit performance. If he has not achieved a sufficient number of correct responses, he may retrace his steps by selecting additional options to continue and improve his learning, and/or refer back to the Behavioral Objectives for a review of the aims and goals of the unit.

If the student has maintained a sufficient number of correct responses, he may proceed to the Attitudinal Objectives, where he may discuss his attitudes about the content of the lesson with his teacher, or he may be guided to a new unit to continue his learning. The Pre/Self Test is self-corrective, thereby permitting the teacher to evaluate the student's performance in the designated unit.

Development of an individualized program requires the evaluation of a vast number of learning variables such as entry abilities of students, numerous learning materials, objectives of the unit, available educative and technological tools, and the results desired. Flexibility, relevance and numerous learning methods and techniques are all key elements in IS Units.

This book does not confine the reader to the development of IS Units only, but provides important substance for the creation of any educational instrument—those already being used in a number of school districts and those yet to be planned and developed. A sample of a variety of these educational instruments is illustrated in the Appendices.

It is my thought that, just as we change and our world changes, so will education change. Consequently, I wrote this book primarily so that others may benefit from these personal experiences with individualized learning through Individual Study Units. I also wrote this book because it is my hope that, perhaps in the future, shared ideas and experiences will produce an instrument even more effective than these Individual Study Units. When this constructive process of change occurs, I will know that my work in producing this book has been worthwhile.

James Lewis, Jr.

Acknowledgements

A special debt of thanks is due to my loyal Special Assistant, Yvonne Carrington, who labored at the Sisyphean task of going through my written materials to help me produce a readable manuscript. I also owe my invaluable secretary heartfelt gratitude for the many hours she spent helping me meet the publisher's deadline.

To James Butler, Elementary Principal of the Milton L. Olive Elementary School in Wyandanch, New York, and John Klein, Project Director of the Individual Study Units Program at Wyandanch Public Schools, Wyandanch, New York, I owe a large measure of thanks for their professional assistance and advice which enabled me to improve my initial draft. No less sincere appreciation and gratitude do I offer to those several teachers in the Wyandanch School District who were responsible for the first hundred Individual Study Units completed and who have spearheaded attempts to individualize instruction in the Wyandanch Public Schools. I feel that I should invoke one of the Muses to inspire me with special words to thank Marcia Rosenstein, a member of the professional staff in the Art Department of Wyandanch Public Schools, who generously applied her creative talent and skills during many extra hours to help illustrate the Individual Study Units so they might be attractive and appealing educational instruments.

Finally, I would acknowledge a debt of gratitude which I know I shall never be able to repay in this life—that one which I owe to my students and their parents who first caused us to focus on creating a viable instrument for the individualization of instruction, and then helped us in the actual development of Individual Study Units by offering constructive criticism and suggestions. Their contributions have been essential to the publication of this book.

J. L.

Table of Contents

Table of Contents

Administering

the Individualized Instruction

Program

1

Organizing for the Preparation
of Individual Study Units

The development of Individual Study Units can proceed only when a careful, logical and organized plan, which embodies implicitness, clarity and viability, has been designed and implemented. When such a plan has been created, the teachers will know what is expected of them; the Project Director will be able to provide adequate guidance and directions; and the resulting product will be a well-designed and developed unit of individual study which will serve as a concrete basis for an individualized instructional program. The intent of this chapter is to provide an outline of the job description of a Project Director; to delineate necessary steps leading to involvement of the Curriculum Council in the projects; to elucidate on methods of training and academically equipping teachers so that they will be adept at planning and developing Individual Study Units; and to discuss the establishment of a publications department which will efficiently produce the finished Individual Study Units.

Step I. Get Initial Approval from the Board of Education

Initially, the Chief School Officer should present the concept behind the utilization of Individual Study Units as a means for individualizing the instructional program. The presentation should not be too lengthy and complex, but should consist of a brief presentation with terse explanation regarding the various components of IS Units.

The next step for the Chief School Officer is to get approval from the Board of Education to grant credits for a teacher in-service course to be conducted on the development of Individual Study Units. The Chief School Officer should then set up a format for the teacher in-service course and publicize the course throughout the schools. A recommended announcement is illustrated in Appendix H. The course should be taught by the Chief School Officer or the Director of Curriculum and Instruction. An example of Individual Study Units for the in-service course is illustrated at the end of this book.

Step II. Establish the Position of Project Director

A school district which intends to implement an educational instrument to facilitate the individualization of instruction must appoint a Project Director to be the overseer of the project. He will be primarily concerned with ironing out the "kinks" while the project is being implemented. It will also be part of his responsibility to guide the staff in the development of Individual Study Units.

The Chief School Officer should select a creative person for this position who will be in charge of directing the program of individualization of instruction. Through his leadership, resource persons within and outside the school may be unified for concerted efforts to revise the present curriculum from group teaching to individualization of instruction. His chief responsibilities would be:

1. To learn the format and become knowledgeable in all aspects of Individual Study Units.

2. To keep the Chief School Officer informed of various thrusts and directions in the development of the Individual Study Units through personal contact and through minutes of the meetings with teachers and students.

3. To keep abreast as a generalist of the latest developments in education affecting Individual Study Units, such as new educational technology, new techniques and methods, etc.

4. To work closely with elementary and secondary supervisors and administrators in implementing Individual Study Units.

5. To examine new research and new ideas in curriculum.

6. To designate units to be assigned to teachers.

7. To be directly in charge of the Evaluation Committee on Individual Study Units. The purpose of this Committee is to examine each completed Individual Study Unit for either recommended changes or publication for use.

8. To establish a follow-up program on the Individual Study Units which are already in use with a view toward possible alteration for greater effectiveness.

9. To establish a plan of operation for the completion of the Individual Study Unit so that the timetable will be commensurate with the opening day of school.

10. To prepare and project the budget for Individual Study Unit development.

11. To be the chief school district representative to meet with parents, community groups, educators and other persons interested in the content, development and purposes of Individual Study Units.

12. To maintain a resource area housing materials, supplies, audiovisual materials and equipment for possible use by teachers.

13. To maintain records of teachers who have completed Individual Study Units, and to authorize payment of fees for such units.

14. To work closely with personnel directly responsible for layout and publishing of each Individual Study Unit, such as the Educational Communications Aide and the printer.

15. To establish a committee of teachers and students for updating the Individual Study Units.

16. To devise all the necessary guides, pamphlets and forms that are necessary for the implementation and the dissemination of information about the program.

Step III. Organize a Curriculum Council

If a Curriculum Council has not been formed, immediate efforts must be expended to organize a ten to twelve member Curriculum Council composed of teachers and supervisors. The Curriculum Council can be organized by requesting the staff to appoint a building representative from each of the district's school plants who will be on the council for the purpose of making recommendations elicited from the staff for the improvement of the project. The Curriculum Council is also responsible for establishing procedures by which the Individual Study Unit project is to be initiated. In this capacity, the Curriculum Council will decide how extensively the program should be implemented in the district. The Curriculum Council has an added responsibility of presenting the program to the community by utilizing a number of efforts such as conferences, film presentations, news articles, etc. The Curriculum Council acts as an advisory council from which the Project Director initiates his activities and makes his recommendations for the improvement of various aspects of the project. Specifically, the tasks of the Curriculum Council would include approval of the concept of individualization of the instructional program by *an instrument.* In order to do this effectively, several steps must be taken, i.e.:

    a. An administrator or supervisor who is thoroughly familiar with Individual Study Units should make a presentation to the Council to explain and demonstrate the use of the units.

    b. Members of the Council should be granted release time to visit schools which have implemented a concept of individualization of instruction.

    c. Teachers who have visited the above schools should return with materials to be put on display for other members of the Council, faculty, students and community members.

    d. A final presentation should be made to the Curriculum Council by a representative designated by those members who have made school visitations.

Step IV. Get Teachers Involved

Even if the Curriculum Council is satisfied that the project is a worthwhile educational venture, it cannot be successful unless teachers are involved and support the concept and the project. Unfortunately, one of man's basic human traits is selfishness and teachers are only human, with selfish tendencies. No matter how much we stress to teachers that this program will improve learning for all students, this will not suffice to arouse teachers' wholehearted enthusiasm for the project. We must appeal to the basic humanity of all teachers—to their generally recognized desire to excel in the field they have chosen—and we must stress to them the impossibility of undertaking any new program successfully without the important support which they can lend. Each teacher's very own self, creativity, ego and vitality must be brought to the forefront and used to help nurture the project. Therefore, the basic task of the administrator or the supervisor is to convince the teaching staff that the instrument will aid and support their functions as educators. Once teachers are assured of this concept, they will eagerly embrace the idea. Several methods may be utilized to achieve this reaction:

    1. Secure literature from various school districts which have implemented a similar program and make it readily available to the teaching staff.

    2. Schedule workshop sessions to discuss and deal with various methods for developing varied Individual Study Units. The I/D/E/A Material Center in Laguna, California, will make available to any school district the services of an expert at a nominal

rate to help supervise a program for developing UNIPACS. A recently incorporated organization, Individualizing Teaching and Learning: Worldwide Association of Provo, Utah, headed by Dr. Glen F. Ovard, serves as a resource to aid school districts which require outside help to assist them in their programs for individualization of the instructional program.

3. A series of videotape films may be obtained from various sources to enlighten teachers on the subject of individualization of instruction. The following list, while not comprehensive, may be of some help:

"Individualization of Instruction and UNIPACS" by Dr. Glen F. Ovard, Dr. James E. Smith, Dr. J. Lloyd Trump and Dr. John Goodlad. Videotape film (Concord 1/2"), from Materials Center of I/D/E/A, 730 North Euclid St., Suite 304, Anaheim, California, 92801.

"Answers and Questions" by Dr. J. Lloyd Trump, 16 mm. film from N.A.S.S.P., 1201 16th St., N.W., Washington, D. C. 20036.

A sound filmstrip on the development of Individual Study Units may also be obtained by contacting the following:

ISU Project Director
Wyandanch Public Schools
Wyandanch, New York 11798

4. Kits and information on how to develop an instrument for individualizing the instructional program may be obtained by writing to any one of the schools listed in this book.

Step V. Get Parents Involved

No matter how well planned a program may be, if parents and community members are not a part of that program, particularly in today's contemporary society, the program cannot progress steadily to success. There are several approaches which may be taken to involve parents:

1. Invite a noted speaker to appear before parents and elaborate to them the necessity, methods, costs and results of individualizing the instructional program. In this area, the aforementioned Individualizing Teaching and Learning: Worldwide Association can be most helpful.

2. Allow parents to examine materials and instruments used by various school districts for individualizing the instructional program.

3. Provide parents with a visual observation of different facets of

various individualized programs on videotape, filmstrips or 16 mm. films.

4. Make provisions for parents to visit various schools implementing different instruments to individualize the educational program so that they may make personal observations.

5. Solicit the formation of a parent team which can help to prepare materials for the development of Individual Study Units.

Step VI. Construct an Organization and Flow Chart Booklet

Arrange to have an Organization and Flow Chart Booklet developed as recommended in Chapter 3. This booklet should be distributed to all teachers involved in the workshop and should be used to designate the particular skill and level to which the teacher will be assigned.

Step VII. Contract with Teachers to Develop Individual Study Units

A memorandum should be circulated among staff members requesting affirmative indication from those who are interested in being employed during the summer vacation to develop Individual Study Units. An example of a suitable memorandum for this purpose is illustrated in Appendix I.

There are two plans which might be used in remunerating teachers for these activities. The first, a "Guaranteed Wage Plan," operates in the following manner:

A number of teachers are selected and retained to work five hours per day, five days of the week, for six weeks over the summer to develop Individual Study Units. A suggested contract and agreement form is illustrated in Appendix J. These teachers are given a "guaranteed" wage, such as $100.00 per week, regardless of the number of Individual Study Units they produce. However, twelve $50.00 units serve as a quota for the guaranteed wage and any teacher who completes in excess of this number receives additional remuneration for each excess unit according to the value of the unit.

The second plan is predicated on the retention of a number of teachers who are willing to work on their own time either in a resource center or their homes. They do not receive a "guaranteed" wage nor are they bound by stipulated hours of work in a specific location, but instead are simply remunerated for each acceptable and completed unit they submit.

Step VIII. Establish a Resource Center

A resource room should be created so that all educational technology, furniture, books, materials, supplies and equipment which are necessary to develop Individual Study Units will be immediately available for use by teachers. The illustration in Figure 1-1 depicts the variety of furniture, equipment, materials and supplies which should be available in this room.

Area A consists of two large tables situated tangentially to the walls of the room. Software, such as textbooks, workbooks, pocket books, projection screens, etc. may be stored here.

Area B accommodates the Project Director's desk and chair with additional seating space for teacher conferences.

Area C is the location in which a large display board may be placed to illustrate the Organization and Flow Chart so that the Project Director may refer in a moment's glance to the specific Individual Study Units which have been completed as indicated by the coloring of completed Levels and Skills.

Areas D and E accommodate two secretaries primarily engaged in retyping Individual Study Units which have been approved by the Project Director. (One secretary is using the primary typewriter and the other is using the pica type.)

Area F houses small bins in which the secretaries may place and store completed units in separate compartments.

Areas G, N and O contain work tables where teachers may work on the Individual Study Units they are preparing.

Area H is supplied for the use of the Art Teacher in developing mini-units, covers and the illustrations for the content of the Units.

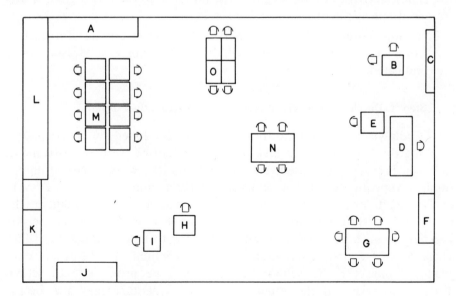

FIGURE 1-1.   INDIVIDUAL STUDY UNITS RESOURCE ROOM

Area I serves as a working area where two or three students may be engaged in cutting out cartoons, pictures, charts, etc. from magazines and discarded books. These students will work closely with the Art Teacher.

Area J contains another bin which the Art Teacher may use to house completed art work.

Area K contains bins which are to accommodate the completed (art work and narrative) Individual Study Units. Each section of the bin may be marked to illustrate the title of the Unit.

Area L houses a large table where educational technology and other equipment may be stored for instant use by teachers.

Area M contains an individual study carrel for those teachers who prefer to work independently away from the group.

Step IX. Get Students Involved

Today's youth demand an active voice in their school program. The development of Individual Study Units offers an excellent opportunity for total involvement by students in their educational venture. There are several methods by which this may be accomplished.

1. Form student teams to work on various sections of the Individual Study Units. Various subteams can be then organized for the tasks of writing materials, adding supplementary cartoons and photographs, and assisting various teachers in a variety of duties. These activities should begin in the initial steps of the program and continue as the program progresses.

2. Various students should be used as "sounding boards" for each completed unit to determine what revisions might be necessary or indicated.

Step X. Develop Audio-Visual Aids to Help Explain the Program

Audio-visual aids for future use may be developed simply by photographing the teachers' work area, the component parts of the instrument, and then preparing a unified script to describe the whole series of photographs. Appropriate editing, splicing, additions and deletions will eventually result in a well-produced audio-visual aid to supplement the program. All staff members in relevant subject areas, such as the Art Teacher, could be utilized as resource persons to help produce the films. There are, of course, commercial companies which may be retained to produce films for the school but this may be prohibitive to school districts, in terms of the expense involved. Videotape may also be experimented with by school districts in the production of these visual aids.

Step XI. Get Final Approval from the Board of Education

The Project Director and the teachers should jointly prepare a presentation to the Board of Education to obtain final approval of the program. At this presentation meeting, printed Individual Study Units should be exhibited to Board members while an enlarged Organization and Flow Chart should be conspicuously displayed. All teachers who have completed the in-service course and who have been involved in the development of Individual Study Units should be present to provide information about and support for the program.

It is to be expected that members of the Board of Education will have a number of questions to ask, the responses to which should be made jointly by the Chief School Officer, Director of Curriculum and Instruction, the Project Director and teachers who have helped to develop and utilize Individual Study Units.

SUMMARY

If the implementation of the Individual Study Units is going to be successful, a foolproof plan of organization which is systematic and takes all exigencies into account must be devised. The organization strategy must cover not only development of the Individual Study Unit, but must also extend to the methods, activities and ways in which all school and community personnel are to be involved, as well as appropriate arrangements for physical plant allocations to house working areas.

It is important for the Chief School Officer to get approval from the Board of Education, parents and the faculty. This can only become a reality if there is involvement on the part of all concerned. Teachers should be used in the development of Individual Study Units according to their abilities, interest, creativity and experience. Because of the variance in aptitudes which will exist, some units will be developed better than others. It is the task of the Project Director to scrutinize each unit in order to improve its effectiveness.

2

Developing
Individual Study Units

Many schools throughout the nation attempt to individualize or nongrade their instructional program, only to eventually fall back into the rut of teaching smaller groups of students as opposed to teaching individuals. The task of providing an individualized instructional program which meets the unique needs of every student in a classroom, using the standard textbook as the basic tool, is not only extremely difficult, but physically an impossibility for any teacher. Even where teacher aides are retained to assist the teacher, the task remains just as herculean. Those schools which have attempted to individualize their instructional programs have necessarily tried to meet a number of problems which were inherited from the traditional educational program. Let us review them:

1. The inability of the teacher to meet the unique needs of each boy and girl in the classroom within a given period.
2. The difficulty of placing each student at his appropriate placement level in a given subject area while using the conventional textbook.
3. The complex task of providing a grouping plan which is appropriate to the needs of each student.
4. The assumption that students will know what they are to do and learn implicitly.
5. The failure of some students to know what behavior is expected of them before or after the presentation of the lesson.

6. The failure of the school to provide adequate measures for the student to evaluate himself while he is pursuing his instructional program.

7. Inadequate testing measures and procedures for the teacher to determine whether or not the student is thoroughly familiar with the content so that he may proceed to another area of study.

8. Frequent presentation of irrelevant books and materials which do not help to reinforce learning.

9. Insufficient opportunities for the student to select what and how he is going to learn.

10. Poorly constructed tests which frequently do not measure what the student was supposed to learn.

11. Neglecting attitudes as reinforcements to learning.

12. Evaluating students only as a means of determining right or wrong answers.

It would seem appropriate at this point to stress that by whatever means we employ to individualize the instructional program we must eliminate most, if not all, of the problems cited above. We might now equate education with the activities of the space agency. The space agency had an objective to land a man on the moon within a certain period. In education, our goal is to individualize the educational program to meet contemporary demands. The space agency had numerous scientists pinpoint the various problems which might be encountered so that once a space ship was built to travel to the moon, it would be capable of surmounting most, if not all, of the problems inherent in space travel. Such is the case with education. Our problems had been enumerated for us, but, the task remained of devising an educational instrument structured as carefully and courageously as the space ship, which could be successfully directed toward an educational program to facilitate learning and teaching. The journey to the moon was successful. The journey through an individualized instructional program can be just as successful. Try it.

DEVELOPING INDIVIDUAL STUDY UNITS

The following pages contain the recommended format for the construction of Individual Study Units. Where the type is in Roman face (this type) the material is to be included in the Individual Study Unit. If the type face is italic *(this type)* the material is presented only as an explanation for the benefit of the reader and the producer of the unit and should not be written into the finalized unit.

    Note: The following material has been placed on separate pages to illustrate exactly how it should be typed and printed.

CONTENT AREA

The cover of the Unit usually contains an attractive design. Somewhere near the bottom of the Unit is the school's identificatory Individual Study Unit mark, together with the name and address of the school district.

The Content Area describes the course area of the Unit. Next is the subheading of the Unit, followed by level designation and the skill or concept. This information is obtained from the Organization and Flow Chart Booklet.

EXAMPLE:

Language Arts/Social Studies

Study Skills
Vocabulary Development
Antonyms

Level D

RATIONALE:

Terms such as Purpose, Reason, Introduction, "What and Why" can also be used to identify the Rationale.

The Rationale should delineate what the Unit is about and why it is important for the student to learn this Unit. There are basically two methods for writing the Rationale, as outlined in Chapter 4.

EXAMPLE:

In this lesson, you will learn about opposites. For example, our cover displays a very obvious opposite! The use of two arrows, one going up and the other going down. These are opposites. Each arrow goes in a completely different or opposite direction. Learning about opposites is useful to you because it helps you to build up your vocabulary.

BEHAVIORAL OBJECTIVE:

The behavioral objective must be stated in terms of observable performance so that the goals may be adequately evaluated in the Pre/Self Post-Tests. There are three basic components which must be included in writing Behavioral Objectives:

1. *The conditions under which the learner will pursue his learning;*
2. *The performance or act must be delineated, indicating what the learner will be expected to learn;*
3. *Minimum standards must be stated.*

There are two styles in which Behavioral Objectives may be written:

1. *Single Level*
2. *Multiple Level*

For further information on these two styles, refer to Chapter 5. A Word of Caution: Use only verbs which can be evaluated in terms of actual performance.

EXAMPLE:

Given information about opposites and how to pick them out, you should, by the end of this unit, be able to recognize given examples of opposites and be able to make up your own opposites. This should be done with 90 percent accuracy.

PRE-TEST

PURPOSE:

The student should receive an explanation of why he is taking the Pre-test. He should be advised that the purpose of the Pre-Test is to determine how much of the lesson to be learned he is already familiar with and what, if any, additional materials contained in the Unit require his further study. The student should also be informed of the minimum number of correct responses necessary for his satisfactory completion of the assigned unit and subsequent assignment to a new unit.

EXAMPLE:

The purpose of this Pre-Test is to find out how much you already know about antonyms.

INSTRUCTIONS:

In view of the fact that one of the functions of the Individual Study Unit is to relieve the teacher of picayune duties, the instructions must inform the student of what he is to do and where he should go to have his test evaluated—either to the teacher, a teacher aid, or a tape recorder.

EXAMPLE:

Ask your teacher for the Pre-Test for this IS Unit. Complete the Pre-Test, then have your teacher evaluate your Pre-Test. She will tell you if you are to continue with this IS Unit.

THE PRE-TEST:

The Pre-Test should be constructed to examine the Thought Process or Thought Derivative which is to be realized through the Behavioral Objective, i.e.: If the Behavioral Objective is constructed so that the Thought Process of Synthesizing is to be realized, then the various test questions should be so constructed.

The format for the various tests may be:

1. *Multiple Choice*
2. *Matching*
3. *True and False*
4. *Completion*
5. *Essay*

LEARNING EXPERIENCE

The Learning Experience is usually a short narrative about the Unit of Study. It is meant to whet the student's appetite for learning. It is in this section that the teacher directs the learning so that it is related to the realities of the student's life experience. The experience can be a short story, an analogy, a poem, a description, an explanation of something, or an article written by a student or parent. The Learning Experience should be so constructed so that if the student did not go any further in his Unit, he should be able to complete the Behavioral Objective successfully. The Learning Experience should be short and to the point. An Experience of more than four typewritten pages may be too long, except in rare circumstances.

EXAMPLE:

You must try to understand that "opposites" mean things that are completely different.

Look at the small book of opposites that goes with this unit. Notice that each picture is completely different from the other one. These are what we call opposites. In the first picture, you see a tall "sky-scraper" building as compared to a short white building. These are opposites. In the second picture, you see the obvious difference between a fat man and a thin man, and in the third one, you see an old stucco house as compared to a new modern house.

Now you pick out the opposite in the last three sets of pictures.

SELF-ASSESSMENT TEST

PURPOSE:

The student should receive clear instructions as to the purpose of the Self-Test or Self-Assessment Test. The basic function of this test is to enable the student to check his progress as he pursues his Learning Experience.

EXAMPLE:

The following contain "Key" questions by which, if answered correctly, you will be able to successfully complete this unit.

INSTRUCTIONS:

In this section, the student may be directed to a scoring key booklet or a tape recorder to check his responses to the Self-Test. The learning system is enhanced when the student has immediate opportunities to check, correct and evaluate his own progress. In a program of individualized instruction which incorporates opportunities for self-testing in individualized study instruments, the tendency to cheat on an examination decreases to a minimum because it serves no useful purpose.

EXAMPLE:

Don't try to answer all of the questions at one time. Do each question when you feel that you can answer it correctly.

SELF-ASSESSMENT TEST

Usually only two or three formal questions are asked of the student. All questions are geared to determine whether, as well as the extent to which, the stated Behavioral Objectives have been achieved.

EXAMPLE:

1. What are ANTONYMS?
2. Write an Antonym for the following:
    A. Man_____
    B. Earth_____
    C. Black_____

LEARNING ACTIVITY OPTIONS

INSTRUCTIONS:

The instructions should specifically delineate how the student is to proceed in his Learning and what will be required of him. The student should be asked to check in the appropriate space those Learning Activity Options which he has selected. The student should be asked to complete no more than 40 percent of the total number of Options available.

EXAMPLE:

Choose any two of the following learning activities to complete.
Place a check (✓) on the line in front of the two you choose.

CONTENT:

Diverse Learning Activity Options must be presented in order to meet the varied and unique characteristics of each student. In this section, students should be given a variety of Options to complete, utilizing a number of different materials, techniques, books, events and equipment. Refer to Chapter 8 for examples.

EXAMPLE:

1. Write five pairs of sentences using opposites.
2. Draw pictures of four or five pairs of opposite words and label them. Do this on a separate sheet of paper.
3. Draw up a list of five pairs of opposites to be placed in two columns. Have a friend take the quiz and then go over it with him.

POST-TEST

PURPOSE:

The purpose of the Post-Test is to determine whether the student has achieved the desired behavior within the prescribed minimum standard as specified by the Behavioral Objectives. The Post-Test is also designed to discover whether the student should be re-cycled back through the Unit, or directed to proceed either to the Attitudinal Objectives or another Unit. A key to the Post-Test is usually kept in an answer booklet for use by the teacher or teacher aide.

EXAMPLE:

The purpose of this Post-Test is to find out how well you are able to complete the objective(s) of this unit.

INSTRUCTIONS:

The Instructions should be framed with extreme clarity, designating exactly what is expected of the student, as well as the location in which he may find a key or where he must go to have his Post-Test scored.

EXAMPLE:

When you think that you have successfully completed this unit, ask your teacher for the Post-Test.

THE POST-TEST:

The Pre-Test and the Post-Test usually measure the same things, but the test questions are constructed differently in order to avoid duplication.

EXAMPLE:

1. A word that is completely different is called an

_____

2. Pick out the opposites and rewrite them in pairs.

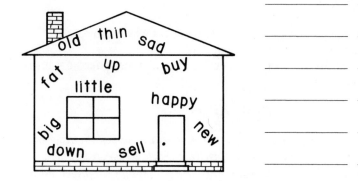

ATTITUDINAL OBJECTIVES

PURPOSE:

The purpose should explain to the student that he is being called in to express his feelings about this IS Unit. There should be no indication that there is a right or wrong answer.

EXAMPLE:

How do you feel about opposites? Let's find out.

INSTRUCTIONS:

The instructions should indicate what the student performance is to be in order to elicit his attitude about the lesson under study. There are three basic ways in which this may be accomplished.

1. Goals and Objectives
2. Examination Questions
3. Learning Experience

Some words indicative of the formation of attitudes include those like faith, feeling, appreciation. Refer to Chapter 9 for additional assistance. The reader must bear in mind that attitude is extremely difficult to evaluate. The primary function of the Attitudinal Objectives section is to provide the student with a broader perspective on which to base his own attitude.

EXAMPLE:

Write how you feel about each of the following:

Avoid yes or no answers.

CONTENT:

EXAMPLE:

1. Do you feel it is important to learn about opposites? Why or why not?
2. Would you care to know more about opposites?
3. Do you feel that, on your own, you might, at some time, make up a list of opposites just for fun?

EVALUATION

Catch-words and phrases should be denoted here as a clue for the teacher to determine if the student has acquired the behavior which is expected of him.

The teacher should also denote here periodically anything unusual as she observes and relates to the student. Comments about the student's attitude may also be stated in this section.

EXAMPLE:

COMMENTS:

Does the student understand antonyms?

Does the student know how to write opposites?

LIST OF MATERIALS

The last page of each IS Unit should contain a list of materials needed in order for the students to complete this Unit and the location in which they can be found.

EXAMPLE:

Materials	Location
1. Book: *Open Highways,* Book 4	Classroom
2. Picture book: *Book of Opposites*	ISU Room
3. Filmstrip: *Africa to America*	Learning Center
4. Shoe Box	ISU Room

GUIDELINES TO EXPEDITE THE DEVELOPMENT
OF INDIVIDUAL STUDY UNITS

The development of Individual Study Units must be accomplished through a systematic approach, so that each unit has all the essential features which are necessary to produce maximum results from the students. There are two forms which help to produce these results:

The Individual Study Unit Outline Form, illustrated in Figure 2-1, is designed to be used by teachers before the design, preparation and completion of an Individual Study Unit. This Outline Form is meant primarily as a teacher guide and reminder during the development of the Unit. In particular, it is basically a guide for each of the component parts to the individual study units which, if the teacher follows it, both facilitates and expedites the development and completion of the Individual Study Unit. On the form are all the essential elements to be contained in each of the components for the teacher to check off as he makes decisions to use particular methods (Terse Method, Introductory Method) or various Thought Processes or Derivatives (Remembering, Classifying), and/or to annotate upon completion of a particular component.

The Individual Study Unit Evaluation Form, illustrated in Figure 2-2, is meant to be completed after an initial draft of a unit has been presented to the Project Director. The latter then uses this form to evaluate the essential elements of the Unit to avoid omissions or incomplete components. This Evaluation Form is primarily a guide by which the Project Director can determine whether or not any given Study Unit will be effective by virtue of adhering to certain elements or components as presented in the Outline Form, and comprehensively developing a final Unit which conforms to the objectives sought. The Project Director will find this form extremely valuable because it provides him with a systematic method of evaluating the Unit and serves to inform the author of the Unit of those areas in need of strengthening, as well as those areas which may be strong, but need more integration with the general subject matter of the Unit.

STEPS IN WRITING INDIVIDUAL STUDY UNITS

A teacher beginning to write IS Units would proceed as follows:

1. Take an in-service course on how to write IS Units to become familiar with the philosophy and format of IS Units. This course should entail practice in writing Units.

2. Consult the Organization and Flow Chart to pick a topic on which to base a Unit. The Project Director may suggest a topic from the chart or may leave it up to the individual to decide.

3. Check the topic with the Project Director who will then decide on the advisability of proceeding with the topic. It may be that the subject matter has been covered in other units, or there may

be a greater need for units on another topic. The final choice of topics is then recorded along with the person's name.

Once the topic has been decided upon, the author develops the Unit in the following manner:

4. Complete the Individual Study Unit Outline Form.
5. Develop the rationale for the Unit, incorporating exciting material, especially materials dealing with the community.
6. Determine the *Behavioral Objectives* of the proposed Unit. Consult the textbook series on the grade level of the proposed Unit, as well as any other pertinent material. The objectives of the texts must be translated into behavioral terms.
7. Write the *Learning Experience*, drawing upon a variety of sources, including students and teachers in the school, textbooks, etc.
8. Compile *Learning Activity Options* based upon audio-visual material, library books, field trips, etc.
9. Devise a series of questions for the *Pre-Test, Self-Assessment Test,* and *Post-Test* that are directly related to the behavioral objectives.
10. Write several questions determining *Attitudes* on the part of the student, and then write the teacher *Evaluation* page.

Having completed a rough draft of the Unit, the following steps are taken:

11. Submit the draft to the Project Director for preliminary evaluation.
12. If no revisions are required, then the Unit is accepted and the author is free to proceed to another Unit. If revisions are required, the Unit is returned to the author along with an IS Unit Evaluation Form which indicates revisions to be made. A conference with the author may or may not be required at this time. Once the revisions have been made, the Unit is accepted.
13. The completed Unit is then added to the list of completed IS Units.

Note: Some school districts may wish to include a teacher's section. This is certainly advisable, particularly when a district is implementing an educational instrument for the first time. All UNIPACS are supplied with a teacher's section and should be referred to as a guide. This teacher's section contains Statement of Idea, Learning Objectives, Instructions to the Teacher, Instructions for Evaluation, Answer Keys and Post Evaluation. The writer has not found this section to be mandatory when implementing IS Units, but it has been helpful to some teachers.

REVISING INDIVIDUAL STUDY UNITS

The process of revising Individual Study Units can be divided into three categories: observation and analysis, revision, and follow-up.

Observation and Analysis

1. A selected number of students are encouraged to work in the Resource Center so that the Project Director can observe their progress and spot difficulties. This also gives the Project Director the opportunity to work with the children and analyze their problems.
2. The Project Director meets with the classroom teachers daily to elicit their comments and problems with the IS Units.
3. The completed Units are read by the Project Director in order to analyze weaknesses in the IS Units.
4. A limited number of Units are used and only a few classes should work on them so that more attention can be paid to perfecting the selected Units. When these units have been revised, more should be introduced.
5. When the students take the standardized tests, this will be a further check on the effectiveness of the IS Units.

Revision

1. *Clarification:* Directions should always be clear, so that the student is certain what is expected of him.
2. *Additions and Changes:* Since the IS Units have been written, many new materials and equipment will have been brought on the market which are pertinent and interesting and therefore should be included in the Units.
3. *Deletions:* IS Units should be judged as to suitability. This is determined if the student doesn't understand the colloquial expressions or has difficulty in comprehending what is expected of him. Individual activities and tests should be deleted or changed as warranted.

Follow-up

1. All revisions should be posted on a master copy of the Unit. Minor changes (a word or phrase) are immediately made by hand in all Units. Major changes involving paragraphs, etc., must await re-typing. The re-typed material should be posted into the Units rather than replace the entire page.

2. There should be a chart prominently displayed in the Resource Center listing major changes.

3. Student's reactions to these changes should be watched to determine the effectiveness of the changes.

FIGURE 2-1.   INDIVIDUAL STUDY UNIT OUTLINE FORM

(To be completed by the Teacher before developing the IS Unit)

Teacher _____ Date _____

I. Description of Content Area:
    Subject _____ Subdivision _____
    Level _____ Skill _____
    Description _____ _____
    _____ _____
    _____ _____

II. Describing the Statement of Purpose:
    A. Check off the method which will be used to state the purpose of the unit:
       _____ Terse Method _____Introductory Method
    B. If the Introductory Method is the selection, indicate which of the following will be used.
       Using a:
       _____ Statement _____Quotation_____Example
       _____Chart, Graph, Drawing _____Others

III. Developing the Behavioral Objectives
    A. Check off the style which will be used to write the Behavioral Objectives:
       _____Single Level _____ Multiple Level
    B. What term will be used to help to realize the Behavioral Objectives?

Write	Distinguish	Enumerate	Identify	List
Construct	Compare	Contrast	Recite	Identify
Differentiate	Solve	Devise	Make	Others

    C. Cite the appropriate Thought Process(es) and/or Thought Derivative(s) to be realized:

    Thought Processes   Thought Derivatives

    _____A. Remembering   _____A. Collecting & Organizing
    _____B. Translating   _____B. Criticizing
    _____C. Application   _____C. Summarizing
    _____D. Interpretation   _____D. Hypothesizing
    _____E. Analyzing   _____E. Imagining
    _____F. Synthesizing   _____F. Classifying
    _____G. Evaluating   _____G. Observing
                                     _____H. Others

IV. Constructing the Learning Experience:
    A. How will the Learning Experience be initiated?

_____ Short Story	_____ Anthology
_____ Role Playing	_____ Explanation
_____ Experiment	_____ Others (Explain)

    B. Who will help produce the materials for the Learning Experience?

_____ Teacher	_____ Student
_____ Parents	_____ Others

    C. How will relevance be introduced?

V. Devising Learning Activity Options:
    A. How many options will be presented?

    B. Briefly identify the options.

    C. Will there be ample allowance for assimilating learning experiences and reality learning experiences?

    D. Will grouping procedures be indicated according to options?

VI. Constructing various tests:

    A. Will there be a Self-Test for students to assess their progress through the learning experience?
    B. What types of tests will be used to evaluate whether the Behavioral Objectives will be realized?

IS UNIT EVALUATION FORM   FIGURE 2-2.

Author of Unit   Date:
Title of Unit

CONTENT AREA   **YES NO**

   1. Is the subject area indicated?
   2. Is there a clear description of the unit?
   3. Are levels, skills and concepts indicated?

RATIONALE

   1. Does the unit indicate what is going to be learned?
   2. Does the unit indicate why the student should learn this unit?
   3. Is the language too difficult?

BEHAVIORAL OBJECTIVES

   1. Is the condition indicated?

YES NO

2. Is the Act or Performance indicated?

3. Is minimum standard indicated?

4. Is the language too difficult?

PRE–TEST

1. Is instruction clearly stated?

2. Has a Pre-Test been adequately developed which can truly measure how much the student already knows about the unit?

LEARNING EXPERIENCE

1. Is the Learning Experience relevant to the realities in which the child is experienced?

2. Is the language appropriate to the level?

STUDENT ASSESSMENT

1. Is a self-test provided for student assessment?

2. Is instruction clearly stated?

LEARNING ACTIVITY OPTIONS

1. Is instruction clearly stated?

2. Are there a variety of Options?

3. Are the Options on a variety of levels?

4. Has the Par Factor of Learning been taken into consideration?

POST–TEST

1. Is instruction clearly stated?

2. Does the Post-Test test the Thought Process and/or Thought Derivatives related to the Behavorial Objective?

ATTITUDINAL OBJECTIVES

1. Is instruction clearly stated?

2. Are one word answers avoided?

3. Are the objectives truly attitudinal?

4. Is the language too difficult?

EVALUATION

1. Are catch words or statements indicated in the evaluation section to aid in the evaluation of the unit?

EVALUATED BY: _____

DATE: _____

COMMENTS:_____

SOME BASIC INFORMATION ON THE CONSTRUCTION
OF INDIVIDUAL STUDY UNITS

Before proceeding with the construction of Individual Study Units, there is some basic information concerning the design and layout of the units which should be discussed.

1. The following are recommended type sizes for the various levels:

   a. Primary Level—Primary Type Face
   b. Intermediate and Junior High Levels—Pica Type face
   c. Senior High Levels—Elite Type Face

2. No Individual Study Unit should exceed fifteen pages in length. There is no need to duplicate a textbook. The student should be made to feel as though he can complete a Unit within a short period of time.

3. If at all possible, the cover of the Unit should be of a card stock with an attractive design to captivate and appeal to youngsters. Two colors are recommended and the art teacher and students should be involved in the production of a cover design.

4. On occasion, where students have not yet learned to read the printed word easily, there are sub-units to accompany the basic Individual Study Unit. These sub-units include an Individual Study Unit Picture Booklet and an Individual Study Unit Worksheet. The Individual Study Unit Picture Booklet is a little book containing pictures that help to illustrate a story which the child can listen to on a pre-recorded tape. The Individual Study Unit Worksheet is used by the child after he has listened to the story on the pre-recorded tape and receives instructions to complete certain tests and options in the Worksheet.

5. Individual Study Units which contain pictures, charts, and graphs should, if finances permit, be commercially printed. Macro Units and Is Unit Picture Booklets should be commercially printed or should not be used.

6. To prevent problems with copyright laws, teachers should avoid using materials taken from textbooks or magazines. If such materials must be used, then permission should be requested from the publisher to use the materials, and authors' credits should be clearly denoted.

7. Fasten only the upper left hand cover of each Unit, using a power staple for a firmer hold.

8. Separate the various sections in the following order:

   a. Content Area (Cover)
   b. Rationale-Behavioral Objectives
   c. Pre-Test
   d. Learning Experience—Self-Test or Assessment Test

     e. Learning Activity Options

     f. Post-Test

     g. Attitudinal Objectives

     h. Evaluation

9. A Resource Area should be set up to house the Individual Study Units. Bins suitable for such purposes might be constructed by the Industrial Arts Department or purchased commercially.

CONSTRUCTING TRI-PART INDIVIDUAL STUDY UNITS

For those primary students who are yet unable to read, the tri-part Individual Study Unit is composed of three integrated components, an Individual Study Unit Picture Booklet, the Individual Study Unit Worksheet and the accompanying Individual Study Unit Pre-Recorded Tape.

The Individual Study Unit Picture Booklet contains a story in pictures for children who cannot yet read. The content of this story has been pre-recorded on a tape to which the student listens while following appropriate instructions about turning pages to see what is happening in the story, etc. The Rationale is actually contained in the taped story. At the end of the pre-recorded story, the Behavioral Objective is stated, and the student is then instructed to utilize his Individual Study Unit Worksheet which contains the Pre-Test, Post-Test, Attitudinal Objectives and Evaluation. The Learning Experience and the Learning Activity Options are on tape. All instructions for completion of the above items are given verbally on the pre-recorded tape, with the exception of the Attitudinal Objectives and the Evaluation, both of which are administered by the teacher when the student has completed the Post-Test and is verbally instructed by the tape to bring his workbook to his teacher.

A sample of the tri-part Individual Study Unit Picture Booklet, Worksheet and Script for pre-recording on accompanying tape are illustrated in Appendix A2.

CONSTRUCTING THE MACRO UNIT

This Unit, which is sometimes referred to under "additional learning opportunities" as "Quest," "Lateral Excursions" and "Opportunities for Amplifying Behavioral Change," is a Unit which evaluates the results of a number of Units.

The Macro Unit is usually given to a student who has completed a sequence of Individual Study Units. These Units are generally very broad in scope and, although challenging for the intellectually gifted student, other students can generally do well on them also. While this Unit is very similar to the Individual Study Unit, the following exceptions should be noted:

A. The Behavioral Objective is usually of the Multiple Level type, and the Thought Processes to be utilized are normally in higher categories involving synthesis and evaluation. There may also be a prevalence of Thought Derivatives included in this Unit.

B. The Learning Activity Options generally require the student to perform some act of originality, such as designing and developing a booklet, developing a newsletter, conducting a major experiment, developing a map, etc. The Macro Unit usually contains only three Options from which the student is to select one for completion, either in a group or individually. Macro Units are generally commercially printed and encased in a single-color cover on which the identification "Macro Unit" is affixed. An example of a Macro Unit appears in Appendix A3.

SUMMARY

The Individual Study Unit provides the student and teacher with an instrument for learning and teaching. This instrument should be flexible in content in order to meet the varied needs of each student in the class. Because the Individual Study Unit is a core component of an individualized instructional program, great care must be exercised in its development, design and preparation. Nothing must be left to chance or taken for granted, not even so small a detail as the most appropriate type size to be used in different Units at different levels. Various types and styles of Units should be considered, and the final Units should be carefully designed, both in format and content, to meet varied needs in the particular student population. While the Individual Study Unit is meant to replace the standardized textbook as a basic educational tool, it is in no way designed to replace the teacher. As a matter of fact, the use of teacher aides to assist the teacher seeking to individualize her instructional program with the use of Individual Study Units is highly recommended. The teacher is an integral component of the Individual Study Unit. Her function is not to instruct all children, but only to assist those that need her. Individualization, too, is an essential component of Individual Study Units. Since these Units are devised for individualized, independent study, small group instruction, conferences with peers, teachers and others must be built into the Unit.

3

Constructing the Organization
and Flow Chart Booklet

The development of an instructional program that provides for the varied differences in each student requires a clear knowledge of educational goals. In order to do this effectively, it is appropriate to specify educational goals in terms of behavioral objectives when attempting to individualize the instructional program. Therefore, the function of an educator which is perhaps primary is to change the behavior of a youngster, either by practice and/or experience, so that he is able to display a certain behavior which does not previously exist as a part of him.

In order to define and write behavioral objectives, some kind of guide is needed to delineate the broad goals and the more detailed specific goals. To accomplish this effectively, an Organization and Flow Chart Booklet should be constructed to serve as a reference to these broad and specific goals. The Organization and Flow Chart Booklet delineates curriculum content of a subject area in a sequential manner, identifying skills, sub-skills, concepts and levels of difficulty. The Organization and Flow Chart Booklet provides a ready and efficient referral source to assure that flexibility is built into the curriculum, while insuring that movement in the curriculum proceeds on a continuum. One may wish to look at this Organization and Flow Chart Booklet as a way to guide teachers in the development of behavioral objectives. The following methods are recommended as possibilities which might be employed to develop an Organization and Flow Chart Booklet.

THREE METHODS OF DEVELOPING THE ORGANIZATION AND FLOW CHART

1. Expert-Produced.

Experts in the varied disciplines may be retained to write the entire continuum. Several college professors might be hired to work in their respective areas to accomplish the task of producing an Organization and Flow Chart, or an organization such as Individualizing Learning and Teaching: Worldwide Association of Provo, Utah, can be contracted to produce the curriculum continuum for the school district.

Advantages of This Method:

A. Professionally produced.
B. Not as time-consuming as when the teacher must prepare the continuum.

Disadvantages of This Method:

A. Expensive to produce.
B. May be irrelevant to the realities of the students.
C. Competence of the "expert" could be in question.

2. Teacher-Produced.

Teachers can be retained over the period of the school's summer vacation to develop the Organization and Flow Chart. This may be accomplished by their identification of the major goals followed by an elaboration on each of the major goals which would contain the specific goals.

Advantages of This Method:

A. Teachers are more apt to include only those items they think should be included in the continuum.
B. There is teacher involvement in the total program of developing Individual Study Units.
C. Teachers may be more inclined to incorporate relevance into the continuum.

Disadvantages of This Method:

A. It may be costly to the District.
B. Some teachers may not be adequately trained to work on the committee which is charged with developing the continuum.

C. This method is extremely time-consuming. If a District is interested in implementing an individualized instructional program which utilizes Individual Study Units, it may have to be put off for one, or possibly two years until the teachers can finish the Organization and Flow Chart Booklet.

D. There exists the possibility that some important skill or concept may be omitted by some teachers.

3. Commercially Produced

A number of book publishing firms produce a scope and sequence chart on the content covered by their books. These charts may be collected at no cost in a given subject area, and a group of teachers may make a decision as to which of the commercial charts most closely meets their particular needs. The grades indicated on these charts may be eliminated by substituting, instead, levels of difficulty designated by letters of the alphabet. The subsidiaries of each major component part can be broken down into skill areas. If social studies is the subject area, then concepts can replace skills, although there are certain materials that would be classified as skills in social studies. The following is an example of materials excerpted from the Scope and Sequence Chart of the American Book Company in Language Arts:

Unrevised Form:

    FORM AND FUNCTION
      First Grade
      NOUN
        Plural Form
        Subjective Function

      VERB
        Predicate Function

      ADJECTIVES
        Describing Words

      FUNCTIONAL WORDS
        Auxiliary
        Connective

      Second Grade
      NOUN (Form)
        Plural Form
        Possessive Form

The above materials from the Scope and Sequence Chart, converted to a Level, Skill and Concept Continuum, would look like the following:

Revised Form:

FORM AND FUNCTION

Level A
  Skill I
  Noun
    Plural Form
    Subject Function

  Skill 2
  Verb
    Predicate Function
  Skill 3
  Adjective
    Describing Words

  Skill 4
  Function Words
    Auxiliary
    Connective

Level B
  Skill I
  Noun (Form)
    Plural Form
    Possessive Forms

Advantages of This Method:

1. It is usually comprehensive in scope and sequence.
2. Development extremely expedient, normally only about two days.
3. Inexpensive to produce.

A method may be developed which may involve a combination of all these methods in order to develop a worthwhile continuum which will do the job, consolidating all of the advantages of the three methods. The only precautions which should be considered are:

A. The expert should have had prior experience in writing curriculum continuum.
B. Only teachers demonstrating competence in the particular discipline should be retained to serve on the committee.
C. Perhaps several of the better scope and sequence charts should be used instead on one, so that content which may be omitted in one is included in another.

Disadvantages of This Method:

1. Not teacher proposed, therefore relevance may not be introduced.

2. Content is usually confined to one book.
3. May be too lengthy at times.

DEVELOPING THE BOOKLET

When the continuum has been completed and developed, a typist should be given the task of typing the original copy either for reproduction on stencils for a mimeographing machine, Xeroxing, or having it commercially printed. Instructions for using the continuum should be developed and a Table of Contents should be completed for the booklet. Because of the excessive use to which it will be subjected, the booklet should be bound.

USING THE ORGANIZATION AND FLOW CHART BOOKLET

When the teacher selects the book in which she will initiate the development of Individual Study Units, she should be encouraged to develop Individual Study Units on a horizontal continuum rather than on a vertical continuum. For example, the content in a Unit on study skills is divided into levels and skills. Level A consists of four skills, beginning with Listening. Level B consists of four skills beginning with Listening. In order to insure that there is a gradual increase in difficulty of content, teachers are asked to proceed from level to level in the same skill, instead of developing all the skills under one level. From time to time, the teacher may wish to develop more than one subject area in one continuum. For example, in History and Nature of Language, Level A, the teacher may wish to present two or three subject areas such as Language or Symbols; Letters Representing Sounds of Language; Word Order in Sentences; and Word Order in Questions, all in one Individual Study Unit. However, it may be that she will wish to include only one, such as Language or Symbols. Caution must be exercised in order to avoid presenting too many subject areas which may confuse the student or produce a cumbersome Individual Study Unit.

At the end of the Organization and Flow Chart Booklet, a section should be utilized for designating the Content Area, Level, Skill or Concept and Subject Area which the teacher has selected, all of which should be so indicated by inserting the appropriate identification in the space provided to develop Individual Study Units.

Figure 3-1 indicates a recommended form which should be reproduced several times on a regular page of the Organization and Flow Chart Booklet.

```
CONTENT AREA
Individual Study Units Selective Assignment
CONTENT AREA  SKILL                    LEVEL
_____  ____  _____  ____  _____
_____  ____  _____  ____  _____
_____  ____  _____  ____  _____


_____
Date Completed
```

FIGURE 3-1.

INDIVIDUAL STUDY UNITS SELECTIVE ASSIGNMENT FORM

PRODUCING A MASTER CHART

Once the Organization and Flow Chart Booklet has been developed and formed, the next step is for the Project Director to develop a Master Organization and Flow Chart and mount it on a large board. The board should be mounted in the teachers' workroom, where the Director will keep a record of which teachers are scheduled to complete particular Units. This display should be large enough so that, at a moment's glance, the Director, or anyone else, may see which levels, concepts or skills have been covered.

SUMMARY

In order for teachers to develop Behavioral Objectives, they must be furnished with a guide, which is usually a continuum of the curriculum content in the form of an Organization and Flow Chart Booklet around which the Individual Study Units will be developed. Teachers should build their Individual Study Units from level to level rather than from skill to skill. This is necessary in order for Units to progress according to difficulty.

A master Organization and Flow Chart should be on display in the Individual Study Units Resource Room so that all concerned parties are kept informed continually as to the committee's progress in the development of Individual Study Units.

4

Developing
the Statement of Purpose

During the nineteenth century, when teachers taught some twenty-five to thirty-five students in a one-room school house, a lesson plan consisted merely of notes referring to pages in a textbook for the teacher's reference. As a rule the textbook was usually reserved for the teacher, and for those few fortunate students with parents who found it economically possible to purchase a luxury textbook. A student might consider himself privileged if he was told by a teacher exactly what he was going to learn. It was even rarer for a teacher to explain why a student should learn a particular lesson.

As time passed, traditionally oriented teachers adopted a more sophisticated attitude toward their "notes" and these evolved into a Lesson Plan similar to the following illustration:

COMPARISON
OF
TRADITIONAL LESSON PLAN AND INDIVIDUAL STUDY UNITS

TRADITIONAL LESSON PLAN	INDIVIDUAL STUDY UNITS
1. Tends to be teacher-oriented and is used to facilitate teacher presentation of the lesson to an entire class.	1. Tends to be student-oriented and serves as a guide for the individualization of instruction to each student, as well as a guide for the teacher.
2. General Purpose: tends to answer ques-	2. Rationale: tells the student what he is

TRADITIONAL LESSON PLAN

tion of "what" is to be learned, however, does not spell out "why" it is to
be learned

3. Aims and Objectives: tend to be stated
in non-observable terms and, frequently, cannot be adequately evaluated because they are too general to be
tested in terms of specific questions at
the end of the Lesson Plan.

4. Test: tends to be obscure in terms of
"proving" that Aims and Objectives
have been accomplished. It usually
consists of a summation of the content, often presented in the form of
general questions which hope ulti-
mately to exhibit the attainment of the
Aims and Objectives of the lesson.

5. Materials and Content: tend to be composed of those extrinsic items or equipment to be used by the teacher, and
the information to be conveyed by the
teacher with their aid so that students
can learn the required Objectives or
Aims.

6. Periodic Quiz: used for the teacher to
determine how well the student has
learned the particular lesson presented.

7. Evaluation: tends to be accomplished,
in the final analysis, by the administra-

INDIVIDUAL STUDY UNITS

going to learn, and also why it is
necessary for him to learn this particular material.

3. Behavioral Objectives: readily evaluated by measuring observable student
performance. Clear delineation makes
it possible for the student to know
what he is going to learn from; what
performance is expected from him and
how much he is expected to learn in
order to reach the Behavioral
Objectives successfully.

4. Pre-Tests: are direct, pointed and particularly designed to exhibit accomplishment of the given Behavioral
Objectives.

5. Learning Experiences and Learning
Activity Options: incorporate relevance, and present a variety of materials, methods and techniques. The
Learning Experience is relevant to
what are realities for students and
serves as a guide for the teacher in
presenting content which is also the
"student's content." In addition to
being relevant, the Learning Experience brings both sides of an issue into
focus, avoids a utopian approach and
is geared to common interests.

6. Self-Assessment Test: used as a checkpoint so that the student can evaluate
his own progress as he pursues his
Learning Experience.

7. Post-Test: provides opportunities for
evaluation after each unit of study has

TRADITIONAL LESSON PLAN	INDIVIDUAL STUDY UNITS
tion of a midterm or final examination, after several topics have been completed.	been completed by the student. In this way, directions to proceed if learning has been successful up to this point may be given or, in the alternative, a student is directed to additional options which will strengthen his learning in the unit before going on to a new unit with weak preparation.
8. No comparable feature.	8. Attitudinal Objectives: constitute important elements in the Individual Study Units which are not specifically dealt with in the Traditional Lesson Plan and are taken for granted. The attitudes which a lesson may influence are important and are examined in a number of ways to elicit student attitude about the given content. Included is a one-to-one exchange between teacher and student to discuss, evaluate and re-orient attitudes where necessary.

However, even these so-called "Lesson Plans" did not contain a statement of purpose for learning a given lesson. In actuality, the purpose was usually stated in terms of why the teacher was presenting the lesson, i.e.: "To teach the recognition of verbs and subjects."

In those days, the teacher was an autocratic, authoritarian ruler in a classroom of students forced to sit, listen and learn. Informing students of a reason for this was uncalled for and would probably have been considered absurd. However, today, when impersonal, restrictive, authoritarian traditionalism is facing a forced exodus from the walls of the classroom, so that humanism may invade these walls in its place, some educators and teachers acknowledge the need for students to be informed of a clear statement of purpose for learning a given unit of work. This statement includes an indication to the pupil of what he is going to learn, as well as an indication of why it is necessary for him to learn the given material. Terms such as "purpose," "reason," "rationale" and, sometimes, "introduction" are used to identify the purpose of the lesson.

There are basically two methods or styles for writing Rationales for learning. These are:

I. *The Terse Method Approach* consists of a brief and succinctly worded statement of purpose indicating what lesson is to be learned and why it is to be learned. It is usually free of long, involved descriptions, verbosity, or educational jargon. The following is a good example of a written Rationale or Statement of Purpose using the Terse Method Approach:

Rationale

The purpose of this unit is to familiarize you with correct usage of the definite articles "a" and "an" and to enable you to compose clearly-stated sentences utilizing the appropriate definite article.

Purpose

What —To familiarize you with the parts of speech
Why—So that you may be able to write clearly stated sentences and be able to identify each part of speech.

II. *The Introductory Method Approach* provides a comprehensive method for introducing a statement of purpose to students and may consist of one or several paragraphs. The introduction is first presented to the student, and is followed by a statement of purpose. The Introductory Statement is meant to whet the appetite of the student so that his incentive to complete the Unit is increased. The Statement of Purpose delineates the "what" and "why" of the Individual Study Unit. The following are examples of the Introductory Method Approach for writing the Rationale or Statement of Purpose for a given lesson:

Using a Statement:

Rationale

When an author writes a novel, he is usually attempting to place before an audience a re-creation of his memory, his experience, his desire, his love, his hate, or his particular dream. Every author seeks to set before his audience some element which is entirely personal to him, but may have a general relevance for any other human being. Every author also seeks to use his facility with words to exert a mental power over the reader which will influence the reader to react to the novel as it represents an extension of the author's self.

The purpose of this unit is to analyze excerpts from the writings of several contemporary American novelists in order (1) to identify the personal elements which the author is trying to convey; (2) to compare these elements for their general human relevance to each other as well as to real life situations; (3) to discover in what ways the author is attempting to influence or direct our reactions; (4) to isolate the factors of form, structure and usage which the author employs to make his characters live as extensions of himself so that you may be able to write a critical book review.

Using a Quotation:

Purpose

> O, reason not the need: Our basest beggars
> Are in the poorest thing superfluous;
> Allow not nature more than nature needs,
> Man's life is cheap as beast's.

King Lear

> My daughter!–O my ducats!–O my daughter!
> Fled with a Christian–O my Christian ducats!
> Justice! the law! my ducats and my daughter!

The Merchant of Venice

> If thou dost love, pronounce it faithfully:
> Or, if thou think'st I am too quickly won,
> I'll frown, and be perverse, and say thee nay,
> So thou wilt woo; but else, not for the world.

Romeo and Juliet

The purpose of this unit is to familiarize you with some of the plays of William Shakespeare so that you will be readily able to identify and explain certain passages in terms of their universality. We will read in their entirety and enact certain portions of the foregoing plays.

Using an example:

Purpose

The Principal thinks I work better than the Supervisor.
(ambiguous)
The Principal thinks I work better than the Supervisor works.
(correct)
The Principal has a better opinion of my work than the Supervisor does.
(correct)

When you make comparisons, ask yourself this question: "Does the sentence convey exactly what I want it to say?" As you study the above first sentence, you will see that the comparison is ambiguous, that the sentence has more than one meaning. You should also notice the difference of meaning in the two correct sentences. Either is correct, depending on the meaning you wish to convey. You should know exactly what you want to say, and then find the exact way to say it.

The purpose of this Unit is to help you to convey a comparison statement with clarity, so that you may be able to avoid ambiguous statements.

Using a Graph:

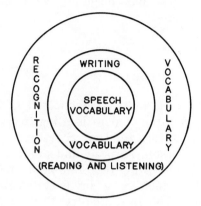

Rationale

The above diagram is a graphic presentation, in concentric circles, of your vocabulary. Notice that the smallest circle, depicting the words you use in speech, is at the center of your entire vocabulary. Around this core, represented graphically somewhat larger, is your "Writing Vocabulary." These two circles represent your *"use"* vocabulary. The large outer circle depicts your "total" vocabulary and involves the words you use, as well as those words you simply recognize.

The purpose of this unit is to increase your vocabulary so that there is a threefold result:

1. It will increase your recognition vocabulary.

2. It will help you to analyze and understand newly recognized words.

3. It will help you to convert words that you only recognize into words that you use.

The reader is reminded that the Introductory Statement is pertinent to the lesson being presented and should denote something interesting and unusual about the lesson in order to arouse motivation. The Introductory Method Approach can be supported with the use of the following materials:

1. Newspapers
2. Magazines
3. Historical Documents
4. Government Publications
5. Teacher-prepared materials
6. Student-prepared materials
7. Parent-prepared materials
8. Poems and prose
9. Books and other reference materials

10. Charts, graphs, tables and diagrams with descriptions or interrogative materials
11. Descriptive Games
12. Puzzles

SUMMARY

The Statement of Purpose must be delineated in all IS Units. This statement must include *what* the student is going to learn and *why* it is important for the student to learn the Unit. Synonyms for the Statement of Purpose are Rationale, Reason, Purpose, and sometimes, Introduction. There are two approaches for writing the Statement of Purpose: (1) The Terse Method Approach, which is a brief statement exploring the Rationale for the Unit; (2) The Introductory Method Approach, which consists of a statement introducing the Unit to the student, and a statement indicating the purpose of the Unit.

5

Identifying
Behavioral Objectives

It is generally agreed that public school teachers do not state educational objectives in behavioral terms. They usually rely on words or terms which are non-observable in terms of behavior and which may contain a wide range of interpretations such as "to understand," "to appreciate," "to realize," etc. Why have teachers failed to write behavioral objectives correctly? The fault for this lies primarily with our teacher training institutions which do not offer courses on the preparation of instructional or educational objectives. However, recently, with increased attention being given to the individualization of instruction, and to many innovative school districts across the country which have come to the forefront in the individualization of instruction, a number of educators and school districts have instituted plans for developing their own behavioral objectives. For example, the staff of one school outside of Detroit has written more than forty thousand behavioral objectives.

DEFINING BEHAVIORAL OBJECTIVES

A behavioral objective is a collection of words, statements, or symbols which describe an educational goal or goals. Behavioral objectives attempt to identify exactly what the student or students should be able to perform at the completion of the unit of work. They are intended to modify or to change learning behavior in the student. But, before we proceed in any depth with behavior objectives, it is best that the reader be made aware of certain items or features which are, in one way or another, related to learning behavior, such as the various types of learning thought processes and thought derivatives.

THREE TYPES OF LEARNING

Whenever a student learns, there are three types of learning which can take place. He can learn for knowledge by acquiring an understanding of main concepts, facts and generalizations with which to organize his information in meaningful and purposeful ways. By doing this, the concepts, facts and generalizations which he acquires and develops will enable him to think critically about any new studies which may arise. He then learns from acquiring attitudes as he improves his thinking. The more he is able to think, using the higher thought processes, the more proficient he will become in learning constructive attitudes about himself and the world about him. The third type of learning which will aid him in his thinking role is skills. Thereby, he is able to obtain appropriate information, process knowledge, and relate this to his previous experiences for solving complex problems.

THE THOUGHT PROCESSES

The seven Thought Processes or the seven kinds of thinking are based primarily on a handbook developed by Benjamin S. Bloom[1] and other scholars, with certain deviations.
In order of difficulty, beginning with the least difficult, there are the following Thought Processes:

I. Remembering:

Remembering is the lowest level of thinking. This process includes the recall or recognition of information previously encountered, such as facts, concepts, or generalizations. This individual knowledge consists of all the information which the student can remember.

Examples of Remembering:
1. He recalls information, such as certain names, dates and places.
2. He can identify the source of materials, such as *Hamlet.*

---

1. Bloom, Benjamin S. (ed.) *Taxonomy of Educational Objectives. Handbook I: Cognitive Domain* (New York: David McKay, Inc., 1956).

II. Translating:

When the student is asked to change information from one form into another.

Examples of Translating:

1. He can translate English into a foreign language.
2. He can write a description of a novel.
3. He can draw a diagram to illustrate a sentence.
4. He can explain in his own vocabulary the meaning of transitive verbs.
5. He can change a story into a poem.

III. Interpretation:

The student uses this thought process to discover relationships between two or more facts, concepts or generalities. It is the kind of thinking which takes place when comparisons are made and conclusions are drawn.

Examples of Interpretation:

1. He can draw a conclusion about the main character after reading a novel.
2. He can compare two or more short stories to decide why they are similar or different.

IV. Application:

When the student can recognize the similarities in new problems to problems previously encountered, and can select the method and the information which is most suitable for finding a solution, he is using the Application Thought Process.

Examples of Application:

1. He can develop a school newspaper or journal.
2. He can apply teaching principles and techniques in a classroom situation.
3. He can use a variety of English skills to prepare a good research paper or oral report on an assigned topic.

V. Analysis:

This thought process is used when the student determines how something is organized. It is used in all kinds of critical thinking and problem solving situations.

Examples of Analysis:

1. He can recognize the point of view of a writer, after reading his book.
2. He can distinguish statements that have no bearing on the questions, or situation.
3. He can separate factual information from theory and conclusion.

VI. Synthesis:

This thought process occurs when the student thinks organizationally or creatively. It is the process of putting ideas and content together to exact a meaningful pattern or stimulus which is new.

Examples of Synthesis:

1. He can write a fictitious novel.
2. He can devise a new method for learning to recognize prepositional phrases.

VII. Evaluation

This is the highest level of thinking for the student. This thought process requires him to use all of the previously mentioned thought processes. In order to evaluate any idea, object, event or person a standard must be the criteria. The standard may have been established by someone else or the individual. The standard must be understood. If it is not, the judge's rule may be faulty.

Examples of Evaluation:

1. He can judge the accuracy and clarity of something read.
2. He can judge a spelling bee contest.
3. He can decide which novel best presents the picture of an angry person.

THOUGHT DERIVATIVES

There is one other facet to the Thought Processes which is not included here. Thought Derivation is the process which occurs when there is an inter-reaction between the highest level of the Thought Process Evaluation and one of the Thought Processes. A list of the Thought Processes which interact to form Thought Derivatives is illustrated in Figure 5-1. While the reader may think of many Thought Derivatives which might be added to the following list, it is not meant to be comprehensive, but rather to stimulate awareness of their existence.

THOUGHT DERIVATIVES

THOUGHT PROCESS INTERACTION

THOUGHT DERIVATIVES	THOUGHT PROCESS INTERACTION
Classifying	Analyzing and Evaluation
Collecting and Organizing Data	Interpreting and Analyzing Synthesizing and Evaluation
Comparing	Interpreting and Analyzing and Evaluation
Criticizing	Interpreting and Analyzing and Evaluation
Hypothesizing	Interpreting and Application and Analyzing, Synthesizing and Evaluation
Imagining	Synthesizing and Evaluation
Observing	Remembering and Interpreting Analyzing and Evaluation
Summarizing	Remembering and Analyzing and Evaluation

FIGURE 5-1.

INTERACTION BETWEEN THE THOUGHT PROCESSES AND THE THOUGHT DERIVATIVES

1. *Classification*—The student can place things in groups according to some principle that we may have in mind.

   Example: He can rearrange a list of words into verbs and predicates

2. *Observation*—The student is able to watch, to note and to perceive.

   Example: He can go to a theatre and watch how the actors take their cues.

3. *Summarizing*—The student is able to state in brief or condensed form the substance of what has been explained or presented.

   Example: 1. After he reads a paragraph, he can state the main idea in one sentence.
                 2. After he listens to a critical analysis about two similar poems, he can describe what was said in a few sentences.

4. *Comparing*—To observe two or more objects, ideas or purposes to determine the relationship between them.

   Example: 1. He can compare one of Shakespeare's plays with one written by another Elizabethan playwright of the same period.
                 2. He can compare his work with that of a neighbor.

5. *Criticizing*—The student is able to analyze and to make a judgment both as to the worth as well as to the defects and shortcomings of a person, place or thing.

   Example: He can write a critical report of a novel.

6. *Imagining*—The student can form an idea about something which is not actually present.

   Example: 1. He can project thoughts as to how life might be in the year 2069 and write a report on these ideas.

7. *Collecting and Organizing Data*—The student is able to gather and examine several sources of information and to collate the findings.

   Example: He can devise a question to be given to a class of students, then collect the answers and write a report on the responses.

8. *Hypothesizing*—The student can pose a statement which may be a possible solution to a particular problem.

Example: He can write a hypothetical statement about something which he thinks is true.

LEARNING: A CHANGE IN BEHAVIOR

Learning is a relatively permanent change in behavior which occurs as
the result of experience or practice. We utilize behavioral objectives to ex-
pedite and direct learning. In order to do this, clearly stated behavioral
goals must be developed. The most important element in writing behavioral objectives is that they must be capable of being evaluated in
terms of observable performance. The terms used should be in active
voice, containing verbs which are capable of being observed and evaluated
by the instructor. Some of these terms are as illustrated in Figure 5-2.

Terms such as desire, feeling, appreciation, values, understanding and
comprehension are difficult to evaluate in terms of observable performance, are attitudinally oriented, and should *not* be used in developing
behavioral objectives.

A well-written behavioral objective should incorporate these
ingredients:

1. It should spell out what the conditions are under which the
   student will perform:
   Example: Given a discussion on the correct usage of subject and
                 verb. . .
2. What specific act or performance will be accepted as evidence that
   the learner has achieved the desired goals.
   Example: you will be able to write ten sentences using subjects and
                 verbs correctly. . .
3. What is the minimum standard expected of the learner.
   Example: with 95 percent accuracy.

The point of concern here is that immediately preceding the
statement of purpose, an instructional aim or goal must be delineated with
a clear and precise description of what the learner must be able to do in
order to demonstrate his accomplishment of the behavioral objective.

For instance, the completed behavioral objective would be:

Given a discussion on the correct usage of subject and verbs, you will be able
to write ten sentences using subjects and verbs correctly with 95 percent accuracy.

TWO METHODS FOR WRITING BEHAVIORAL OBJECTIVES

There are two distinct methods for writing behavioral objectives.

COGNITIVE DOMAIN

REMEMBERING	TRANSLATING	INTERPRETING	APPLICATION	ANALYZING	SYNTHESIZING	EVALUATION
Recognition	Changing the form	Discovering Relationship	Using Knowledge	Taking Apart	Putting Together	Judging
Write	Transform	Explain	Canvass	Compare	Create	Decide
List	Render	Define	Solicit	Distinguish	Make	Resolve
Enumerate	Decode	Construe	Employ	Determine	Form	Form an Opinion
Relate	Decipher	Render		Identify	Devise	Settle
Recall	Transfer	Spell Out		Analyze	Conceive	Discriminate
Recollect	Remove	Elucidate		Select	Propagate	Determine
Retrace	Change	Illustrate		Match	Invert	Discern
Recite	Interpret	Disentangle		Classify	Originate	Ascertain
	Construct	Unravel		Compare	Bring into Being	Investigate
	Transmute	Make Out			Establish	
		Account For				Write a Review
		Clear Up				
		Exemplify				
		Decipher				
		Expound				
		Solve				

Note: Some words may be listed under more than one Thought Process, depending upon how they are used in a particular sentence.

FIGURE 5-2.

SEVEN THOUGHT PROCESSES AND THEIR IDENTIFIABLE TERMS

These are the Single Level Approach and the Multiple Level Approach.

1. The Single Level Approach deals with one single thought process or one single thought derivative.

Example:

A. THOUGHT PROCESS—Translation

Given a book to read and study on the different kinds of sentences, you will be able to write declarative sentences in your own words with 85 percent accuracy.

B. THOUGHT DERIVATIVE—Classification

Given a book to read and comprehend on the different types of sentences, you will be able to distinguish between different kinds of sentences and identify them as Interrogative Sentences, Exclamatory Sentences or Declarative Sentences with 85 percent accuracy.

2. The Multiple Level Approach deals with those behavioral objectives which concern themselves with two or more thought processes and/or two or more thought derivatives and/or one thought derivative.

Example:

A. THOUGHT PROCESS—Remembering, Translating and Analyzing.

Given a book to read and study on the different types of sentences, you will be able with 85 percent accuracy to:
1. Name the various types of sentences;
2. Change Declarative Sentences into Interrogative Sentences;
3. Underline all of the Interrogatory and Declarative sentences.

Example:

A. THOUGHT DERIVATIVES—Observing and Criticizing

Given a book to read and study on the different types of sentences, you will be able with 85 percent accuracy to:
1. Listen to a student's conversation, and write down the number of Interrogatory Sentences used in that conversation;
2. Write a critical review of the book which is used to describe the various kinds of sentences.

If the reader has fully understood this section of the chapter on Behavioral Objectives, he should be able to write clearly stated behavioral objectives which can be evaluated in terms of observable performance. He should also be able to write behavioral objectives that will direct the learner through one or more of the thought processes or thought derivatives.

A FEW WORDS OF CAUTION
WHEN WRITING BEHAVIORAL OBJECTIVES

For years, educators have been writing aims, goals and objectives for their students, only to take the learning process for granted. The author means by this that the Thought Process was not in the least taken into consideration, and if it was considered, most objectives revolved around the lower Thought Process of Remembering which involves primarily the simple process of memorization. In contemporary society, emphasis is given to those Thought Processes which function at the highest levels, such as analysis, synthesis and evaluation.

Instead of a Behavioral Objective like the following:

> Given the seven parts of speech, you will be able to recite all the parts of speech with 100 percent accuracy;

involving only the Thought Process of Remembering, a more preferable Behavioral Objective which includes a higher level of thinking and encompasses the Thought Process of Analyzing, would be more desirable, i.e.:

> Given the seven parts of speech, you will be able to write a paragraph and underline all parts of speech with 100 percent accuracy.

The first Behavioral Objective necessitated only the memorization of the seven Thought Processes, whereas the second Behavioral Objective demands that the student be able to select the proper part of speech to write a clearly worded and functional paragraph.

Another word of caution: The Post-Test must be designed so that it examines the Thought Processes or Derivatives which were to be realized in reaching the Behavioral Objective. For example:

Correctly	Given a unit on the use of the semi-colon, you will be able
Stated	to identify the juncture in these sentences which should
Behavioral	contain a semi-colon, with 100 percent accuracy.
Objective	Explain, in your own words, the function of a semi-colon.

The Behavioral Objective encompasses the Thought Process of Analyzing. The Post-Test question examines the student's ability to translate, which involves the Thought Process of Translation. The following question is appropriately stated:

Correctly	Insert the missing semi-colons in the following sentences:
Stated	Learning can take place without a teacher but teaching
Post-Test	can hardly take place without a learner.
Question	The man on the plane regurgitated he was air-sick.

The Behavioral Objective and the second Post-Test question are "thought related" and, therefore, are appropriately stated.

SUMMARY

The function of education is to change or modify behavior. Behavioral Objectives are designed to indicate the desired behavior; therefore, they can be defined as a collection of words, statements or symbols which describes an educational intent. Students learn to acquire knowledge, attitudes and skills. There are three domains of learning, *i.e.,* the Cognitive (thinking), the Affective (attitude) and the Psycho-motor Skills. Behavior results from thinking and learning. Therefore, in order to write clearly stated Behavioral Objectives, the reader must be able to write these objectives realizing the seven Thought Processes and the Thought Derivatives, so that the aims and goals of the lesson are readily brought out and may be adequately evaluated in terms of the expectations.

6

Tests for Individualization
of Instruction

The evaluation mechanism is an essential feature of the Individual Study Unit. During the process of evaluation, the teacher must use her professional knowledge to make value judgments in terms of adequate performance of the act by minimum standards as stipulated by the Behavioral Objective. The teacher is responsible for evaluating the various tests in the Individual Study Unit. She also makes her evaluation according to what she may or may not see in a student's attitudes and values. The purpose of this chapter is to briefly explain the primary facets of the Placement Test, Pre-Test, Self-Test, Self-Assessment and Post-Test. The author will also present the generally accepted format for evaluation tools which form a part of Individual Study Units, such as "True or False," "Matching," "Multiple Choice" and "Essay." Primarily, it seems wise to devote some discussion to methods of correlating test questions with realization of Behavioral Objectives.

THE PLACEMENT TEST

Before any Individual Study Unit may be prescribed for a student, a Placement Test must be administered to determine at what level, skill and/or concept the student's learning is to be initiated. The Placement Test may consist of either a commercially produced "academic achievement test," or of a transformation of the Pre-Test into a Placement Test. If a standardized academic achievement test is given to determine placement, the educator must be aware that the test might not be referent to all those areas on which the Organization and Flow Chart is based. In such cases, an amendment is indicated. While it is true that there are some excellent commercially prepared Placement Tests in certain subject areas such as Reading and Mathematics, it remains true that for other areas such as Language Arts, Social Studies and Science, appropriate Placement Tests are difficult to acquire. If possible, all of the Pre-Tests may be consolidated and rewritten so that the student is not posed identical questions more than once. Although this is time-consuming, it may be the most ideal method of providing an efficient Placement Test to identify the placement level of a student.

Each subject area should be divided into several components before this task is undertaken. For instance, in Language Arts, separate components might consist of Usage, Form and Function, Mechanics, Composition, Spelling, Study Skills and Proofreading. An imaginary academic achievement test administered to a student might look something like the following:

LANGUAGE ARTS COMPONENT PART	GRADE LEVELS	PLACEMENT ESTIMATED LEVEL PLACEMENT
Usage	6.4	G
Form and Function	8.1	J
Mechanics	8.2	J
Composition	10.1	M
Spelling	11.5	O
Study Skills	10.0	M

A glance at these scores indicates that the student needs to focus on Level G in Usage and at Level J for Form, Function and Mechanics. Therefore, a Pre-Test Level Test should be given to the student to determine the exact areas in each of the three components which require concentration. When the area of concentration has been determined by the teacher, an appropriate Individual Study Unit may be prescribed for the student. The teacher should then initiate instruction in the Individual Study Unit by beginning at the lowest grade or level and proceeding upward until approximately all levels are ranged at the same line of achievement.

FUNCTION OF THE PRE–TEST

A Pre-Test is administered to a student just before he is to undertake the Learning Experience. These test questions are designed to measure the achievement of the particular skill or concept as it relates to the Behavioral Objective. Each sub-division of the Behavioral Objective will be examined by various questions in the Pre-Test. Before the student attempts to complete the Pre-Test, he should first give it a cursory perusal to ascertain for himself whether he thinks it is possible for him to complete it successfully. If he feels that it is too difficult for him to complete successfully, then he should not attempt it. As an example, let's suppose that the student was given an Individual Study Unit which identified the following Behavioral Objective:

Given this unit on effective Organization, you will be able with 90 percent accuracy to:

1. Organize a complete composition, incorporating unity, pertinence, coherence, transitory structure, emphasis and order (Analyzing) and

2. Prepare an outline (Translating).

Appropriate Pre-Test questions must include the Thought Processes of Analysis and Translation. To facilitate this, some appropriate Pre-Test questions might be:

A. Write a short essay of approximately 300 words. Be certain that everything in a sentence relates to everything else in that sentence.

B. Excerpt a paragraph of approximately 250 words from any book, and indicate the purpose or main idea contained in the paragraph.

C. Underline the topic sentence in a paragraph to which your teacher will refer you.

D. Compose twenty transitional words and phrases.

E. Directions: In the following paragraph, one sentence is out of contextual order. Underline that sentence and indicate its proper position by placing a check mark next to it.

The first and last positions in a sentence are the most emphatic. Salient points should be placed in these positions. This rule on emphasis also applies to the structure of paragraphs. The first and last sentences of any paragraph are the most emphatic. Also, the first and last ideas expressed in an essay are given more emphasis. Because of their position, you tend to remember them longer than other sentences in a paragraph.

F. Select a paragraph from any book of about 300 words and prepare an outline of it.

If the student cannot give correct response to at least 90 percent of this Pre-Test, then he is directed to complete the Individual Study Unit.

THE SELF-TEST OR SELF-ASSESSMENT TEST

Actually, these are two tests which serve the same function. They both provide the student with checkpoints so that he becomes able to evaluate his own progress as he proceeds through the Unit. Occasionally, the Pre-Test may be used as a Self-Test. If a Self-Assessment Test is not available, the Pre-Test should be used by the student to evaluate himself while he is completing his Learning Experience. Self-Assessment Tests should usually consist of a few terse questions, such as the following:

1. Explain the following:

   A. Unity and Pertinence
   B. Central Idea Statement
   C. Topic Sentence
   D. Coherence and Transition
   E. Sentence Order
   F. Emphasis

2. Give an example of the following:

   A. Topical Outline
   B. Sentence Outline
   C. Rough Outline

As the student proceeds through his Learning Experience and Learning Activity Options, he periodically takes the Self-Assessment Test to determine whether he can answer the questions in the Self-Assessment Test.

THE POST-TEST

The Post-Test is similar to the Pre-Test. Once again, the Thought Processes or Thought Derivatives must have been utilized and realized in reaching the Behavioral Objectives. If the student achieves the minimum standards stipulated for the Behavioral Objective, he will then be instructed to proceed through the Attitudinal Objectives. When the entire Unit has been successfully completed, the teacher directs the student to another Unit. If the student does not maintain the minimum standard, he is re-cycled through either the Behavioral Objective to refresh his recollection of what is expected of him, or he is directed to complete the remaining Learning Activity Options.

DEVELOPING THE SCORING KEY BOOKLET

A Scoring Key Booklet should be maintained for all Pre-Tests,

Self-Assessment Tests and Post-Tests. This can be accomplished by consolidating the various test answers into three booklets so that they are immediately available for use by either the teacher or teacher aide and the student. Sometimes the Keys are recorded on tape recorders or language masters.

CONSTRUCTING TEST QUESTIONS

There are two types of test items:
1. Objective Test Items, and
2. Essay Test Items.

Objective Test Items

Objective test items may be classified in either of the following categories:
1. Multiple Choice Tests
2. Supply Tests
3. True-False Tests
4. Matching Tests

Multiple choice test questions are composed of incomplete sentences followed by a choice of words or phrases, one or more of which may be appended to complete the sentence correctly.

Example: To have completeness of thought is to have:
   A. coherence and transition
   B. a central idea statement
   C. unit
   D. intensive words for emphasis

The multiple choice test question has been widely used. It is very simple to build into this kind of test question the Thought Processes of Remembering, Interpreting, Analyzing and Synthesizing.

Supply test questions (or statements) are usually incomplete and require that the student supply the appropriate word or phrase which will correctly complete the statement.

Example: Arranging sentences and paragraphs into a logical and sequential order is identified as _____.

These questions usually entail utilization of the Thought Processes of Remembering and Interpreting and tend to be limited in realizing other Thought Processes or Thought Derivatives.

True-False Questions consist of a question or statement which requires only a decision by the student as to its truth or falsity.

Example: (True or False) If two sentences are closely related, they should not be separated by another sentence, or several other sentences.

This kind of question is usually restricted in the number of Thought Processes which may be utilized, but Remembering and Interpreting would certainly be required in arriving at the correct response.

Matching Test Questions usually consist of two or three lists of items and a set of instructions to be followed in matching items from one column with those of another.

Example:

1. A sentence which helps to link parts of a paragraph together is called a	A. Coherence
_____	
2. Analyzing and placing sentences of a paragraph into logical and sequential order is called	B. Transition Sentence
_____	
3. The first and last positions in a sentence are	C. Most emphatic
_____	

This question-style is useful in determining how well students can recall or remember certain information, and the Thought Processes of Remembering, Interpreting, Translating or Analyzing may be used if the items to be matched (first column) are interrelated to one central thought.

Essay Test Items

This test item demands that the student supply the answer to a given statement or question. This response must usually be couched in one or several sentences and this kind of response usually requires a subjective judgment on the part of the instructor. These questions can be constructed to incorporate any of the Thought Processes or Thought Derivatives. Some of the key words used in posing items of this type are "describe," "explain" and "construct."

SUMMARY

Evaluation is an essential feature of any educational program. Part of the preliminary steps leading toward a successful evaluation must include a Pre-Test to be given to the student to determine how much of the content the student already knows and where best to proceed from this point. The Self-Test or Self-Assessment Test must be provided to satisfy the student's interest in evaluating his own progress as he proceeds through the Learning Experience and the Learning Activity Options. The Post-Test, of course, constitutes the final analysis of how well the student has met the stated Behavioral Objective. Where a student has been successful with the Post-Test, it is important that consideration be also given to his achievement of the Attitudinal Objectives presupposed by completion of the Unit, prior to his assignment to a subsequent Unit. If he has not been successful, re-cycling through the Unit or certain portions of it is obviously indicated. For purposes of effective evaluation it is important to delineate the two major test categories:

1. Objective Test Items which include multiple choice test questions, supply test questions, true-false test questions and matching test questions; and
2. Essay Test Items which are subjective in nature and demand an extended reply by the student.

A scoring key booklet should be devised for all Pre-Tests, Self-Assessment Tests and Post-Tests. The scoring key can be recorded on a tape recorder or language master. The teacher, teacher aide and student have accessibility to the scoring key booklet.

7

Writing
Learning Experiences

If the aim is to activate learning in a student, there must be some catalytic element which will initiate the action. In the Individual Study Unit, the Learning Experience is that component part of each Unit whose primary function is to arouse a spirit of inquiry in the student and inspire him to learn a given unit of material. Although this is difficult to do at times because of the wide range of abilities and interests, this is an essential part of the learning process which must be given careful attention. Basically, the core of the Individual Study Unit is the Learning Experience and the Learning Activity Options. The Learning Experience is intended to arouse interest in the student to learn. The Learning Activity Options are intended to maintain that interest. This chapter will explore methods and techniques which have met with some success.

METHODS OF WRITING LEARNING EXPERIENCES

Perhaps the most important function of education is to interest students in learning. In order to do this effectively, the materials introduced to the student must meet several criteria:

1. They must be relevant to the realities which the students are experiencing. To serve this purpose, materials should be written to encompass the following:

    a. *Community*—This includes materials related to the immediate community, such as the home, neighborhood, church, school, public and municipal buildings, as well as professionals, stores, agencies, etc. in the community.

b. *Everyday Life Activities*—These experiences would include any activities which involve matters pertaining to the daily life existence, such as taxes, eating, recreation, etc.

c. *Current News Events*—These experiences would include that information which is broadcast, telecast or contained in the news media which is of general knowledge and interest to the public at large, such as space flights to the moon, children starving in Biafra, the Vietnam war, President Nixon, etc.

d. *General Knowledge*—This area would include those experiences comprising generally accepted knowledge, such as use of the dictionary, following directions, filling out an application form, composing shopping lists, etc.

e. *Basic Life Necessities*—These experiences would include anything dealing with the basic necessities of life common to all human beings such as shelter, clothing, food and drink.

2. There should be ample opportunity for simulated games and socio-dramas with role playing of major characters. It is often difficult to bring real life experiences to the student, therefore, a method which has often met with success and which should be attempted is the simulation of real life experiences. A number of publishers have produced simulated games and this author would be willing to predict that, in the future, simulated educational games will receive much new attention.

3. The language used in the Learning Experience should be both informal and formal. All Learning Experiences should be written in the second person. The teacher should use a duo-lingual technique for activating the Thought Processes of the student. There is no harm in the teacher using the dialect, idioms and slang expressions of the particular community in order to develop the Learning Experiences in the Individual Study Unit. In fact, this procedure is highly desirable, and depending upon the community composition, might include dialectical expressions familiar to Jewish, Italian, black and Irish minority populations.

4. The Learning Experience should not assume a utopian approach which indicates only the positive side of a situation. When this does take place, it distorts the structure and presents an unrealistic view. For years, the standard textbook has been distorting history and, recently, educators are beginning to demand that both sides of the situation be presented. For example, did Lincoln actually declare

war on the South to free the slaves? Was John Brown really a villain? In yesteryear, the answers to both of these questions would decidedly have been in the affirmative. Today, many more sources will reply in the honest negative. It is perhaps true that a more realistic portrayal of the events cited above might have prevented some of the quandaries students often find themselves in with regard to what is right or what is wrong.

5. The "common interest" or "commonality" should be the concept which constitutes a major part of the Learning Experience. Learning is enhanced when the Learning Experience is related to people and places which are familiar to the students. Commonality also insures relevancy.

6. The Learning Experience which is reinforced with cartoons, photographs, drawings, charts and graphs is certainly going to be more captivating to the student for learning than that Experience which relies solely on the printed word. This is particularly true where the illustrated material is related to the community or is commonplace to the student.

7. It is essential, at times, for the Learning Experience to provide opportunities for youngsters to share their ideas and approaches to the subject matter with each other in small groups. The individualization of instruction does not on the surface, but does in its structure, demand that a number of socializing techniques be employed to make learning more viable for the learner.

TECHNIQUES FOR WRITING LEARNING EXPERIENCES

In the section on Methods of Writing Learning Experiences, the author mentioned ways in which experiences can be presented to help arouse and maintain the student's interest so that he can learn. In this section, we will provide the reader with some techniques which may be employed to help develop the Learning Experience, realizing the various methods mentioned previously.

There are basically three techniques which can be used to help develop the Learning Experience:

1. The teacher can be retained to write the Learning Experiences, using as a perceptual base his own experiences with the students and their environmental background. If he is creative, he can develop a Learning Experience which will meet most of the needs of the students. Usually, when they are composed, they are written in instructional terms. However, nothing precludes the teacher from composing Learning Experiences in the form of short stories, events, poems, etc.

LEARNING EXPERIENCE

Every time you open your mouth to speak about a thing you see, or something you hear, you are using words to describe what you see or hear. This is how we talk about differences.

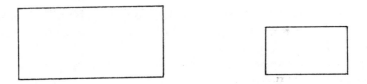

Look at the first two pictures, then read the next two sentences.

1. The box on the left is ————————————————.
2. The————————————————box is on the right.

The words that you would put in the blanks are used to describe. Words that describe things are called *adjectives.* You will be using adjectives to describe many different things. When you do your Learning Activity Options, keep in mind that you should be able to use adjectives, and to know when you are using them.

An Example of a Learning Experience Written
by a Teacher in the Form of an Anecdote:

LEARNING EXPERIENCE

A prefix is a group of letters that can be attached onto the beginning of a word to change its meaning. *For example:* A boy comes to school with his shirt buttoned wrong. His teacher sees this and tells him to unbutton his shirt and then rebutton it properly.

Thus, the teacher has just taken the word button, placed one prefix in front of it to make "unbutton" and then placed another prefix in front of it to make the word "rebutton."

Example: A child has been bad in school and the teacher calls his home in order to speak to his mother. Instead, he speaks to an older sister who tells him she can recall a similar event which happened some time ago.

You have just seen a word "call" with a prefix added to it to make it "recall" which means to call back.

An Example of a Learning Experience Written by
a Teacher in the Form of an Informative Report:

LEARNING EXPERIENCE

A suffix is a group of letters that can be added to the end of a word to change its meaning. *For example:* Every boy at one time in his life goes out to camp in the backyard. He sets up a tent, builds a fire and becomes a camp*er.* As you can see, we have taken the word "camp" and added the suffix "er" to it in order to make a new word.

Another example: A little girl gives her mother some help with the dishes, makes the beds, and vacuums the rugs. She has been a help*er* to her mother who rewards her with one dollar and says, "Thank you, you have been very help*ful* to me." Again, we have taken the word "help" and added the suffixes "er" and "ful" to form two new words.

2. The students themselves may help to develop materials which can be incorporated into the Learning Experience. One method which was tried by a school district consisted of releasing a teacher for two months to collect written materials from students to produce a progressive reading textbook. The teacher met periodically with groups of teachers and presented them with a format of subject areas on which he wanted students to write. Some of the areas included:

What I Like or Dislike About My Community

My Favorite Television Program

The Man: Dr. Martin Luther King, Jr.

The students were instructed from time to time with regard to whether they were expected to write a short story, a script, poem or prose. After the materials were composed by the students, they were instructed to append their name and age to the material before presenting it to their teachers. The teachers, in turn, submitted all of the student-written materials to the teacher in charge of the program and he decided which materials were to be used for publication. Incidentally, the students were informed about the project and demonstrated a great desire to participate. In fact, many of them took their assignments home with them to complete their materials outside regular school hours. To incorporate authenticity, only a few errors were corrected by the teacher in charge. After deciphering all of the student-written materials, they were forwarded to a typist who prepared a final draft. The drafted material was then bound for a twofold purpose:

a. To help develop Learning Experiences; and

b. To publish a progressive reading textbook written by students.

The materials that follow have been used effectively in developing Learning Experiences and can be used to teach sentence structure, reading, development of a theme, or a combination study of spelling, punctuation and a host of other skills:

An Example of a Partial Learning
Experience in the Form of a Story
Which Includes Materials Written
by Students:

TIMMY CARTER

by Calvin Manning

Timmy is a small boy who is always getting into trouble. One day he went into his brother's room and he got some matches and his brother's firecrackers and lit them. POW*–POW*–POW** Timmy had a headache from all the noise.

When his brother came home he yelled at Timmy and scolded him. Timmy went into the basement and he turned on the washing machine. Swish! Swash!–went the machine. Timmy got excited and he hit the machine and broke it all up.

When his mother came home she beat him and beat him. Timmy went outside to his father's car and took a can of orange paint and painted everything.

When his father came home he scolded him so he went into the backyard and took out his sister's bike and he gave it a flat tire.

When his sister came home she yelled at him, Timmy felt sad. "Nobody likes me" he said, then he started to cry.

The next morning, mother asked "Eddie, where is Timmy? I don't know mother, said Eddie. Sue come down here. Yes mom. Have you seen Timmy? No mam. Jimmy, come here, Yes ma. Have you seen Timmy. Well, I saw him last night. I haven't seen him since."

"Mom" Sue called in a heavy noise! Come here quick. Sue found a note on the table. The note read:

Dear Family,

You don't love me anymore. I have gone away.

                                                                        Timmy

"Oh dear, mother said. Eddie, go get your car out. We must go and find him. Sue and Jimmy, you two must stay here and watch the house."

Mother had left in a flash. eeeeeeeee! went the brakes when dad stopped the car. And there lying beside the road was Timmy. "Is he dead? No said a man. He's just asleep. Thank God." said mother.

What's in the big bag beside him? I don't know. Mother looked in the bag.

All of Timmy's clothes and toys were in there. Mother put him in the car and they went home. Timmy woke up and had a lot of fun.

THE END

An Example of a Partial Learning
Experience in the Form of a Prose
Poem Which Includes Materials
Written by Students

THE SNOW

by Marilyn E. White

That's some good snow falling from the sky.
   That's some beautiful snow falling in your eye.
To play in snow is fun.
   To laugh at each other,
Throwing snowballs at each other
   And having a lot of fun playing in the snow.
Falling like a bird
   Dropping out of the sky
And like rain falling on the window pane
   Snow is very good to play in.
But having fun playing in the snow
   Is like playing with a toy
Let's be nice when snow is falling from the sky
   Like rain falling on the ground.
Be nice so you can go out in the snow and play.

An Example of a Partial Learning
Experience in the Form of a Poem
Which Includes Materials Written
by Students:

WYANDANCH IS THE PLACE FOR ME

by Linda Belcher

Wyandanch is so pertty I can't believe my eyes.
   I look up at the bright blue sky,
And watch the cloudy stars go by.
   And then I look upon the world and see
The pertty flowers and the trees
   And I even watch the bees.
And then I say to myself
   Wyandanch is the place for me.
I keep my eye open all the time
   It is so pertty it makes me want to cry
And I look around and say
   Wyandanch is the place I want to be.

In addition to writing materials, students may also be asked to write titles for Individual Study Units and compose drawings which can be used either as covers for certain Units or to add depth to the Learning Experience.

If student-prepared materials are used, students should, at all times, be given credit for their contribution. Students enjoy seeing their names in print and their peers enjoy reading materials prepared by their friends.

3. In certain instances, parents have prepared materials which teachers have found fitting for use in the Learning Experiences section of Individual Study Units. Of course, if the teacher wishes to have parents contribute materials for inclusion in the Individual Study Units, this should be well planned in advance. One method of doing this consists of the formation of a committee of parents who will be involved in writing relevant materials to aid the teaching process. The same techniques which are used to encourage students to write can usually also be used to encourage parents to make their contributions. There are, perhaps, scores of parents who would literally jump at the opportunity to display their literary talents and aid in the instructional program. Like students, and for the same reasons, parents should always be given credit for their contributions.

This technique of utilizing parents to help develop Learning Experiences is a wonderful public relations gambit for the Individual Study Unit project.

SUMMARY

The Learning Experience and Learning Activity Options constitute the core of the Individual Study Units. The Learning Experience arouses interest in learning and the Learning Activity Options maintain this interest. The Learning Experience must be relevant to the realities which the students experience. Educational simulated games and socio-dramas with role playing of major characters should be an incorporated feature of the Learning Experience. The Duo-Lingual Technique should be a major part of the Learning Experience to help arouse interest. The student should be informed of both the negative and positive aspects of a situation rather than only being presented with a positive utopian outlook. Inclusion of the students' community helps to insure relevance. Cartoons, drawings, charts, graphs, etc. all help to nurture the student's opportunities for learning. Socialization is an important factor in the individualization of instruction.

Techniques for writing Learning Experiences should involve the teacher, student and the parent, all sharing in the development of relevant Learning Experiences.

8

Forming
Learning Activity Options

Students vary in many ways as was more fully discussed in Chapter 5 dealing with the subject of Behavioral Objectives. Each boy and girl has unique needs, interests and abilities that must be taken into consideration when an individualized instructional program is contemplated. Students must be fully involved in the learning process if they are to obtain maximum benefits from the educational program. In American public educational systems of previous centuries, the interest component of the learning process was long neglected. Today, however, the interest component must play a central role in any effective educational program. Usually, with the use of a standardized textbook, difficulties of arousing interest among varying students with individual needs was a task left to what was assumed to be an inordinate supply of creativity, time and endurance on the part of the teacher. This, of course, was an impossible task. Study Units which are individualized unburden the teacher to a large extent by providing a variety of interest approaches in Learning Activity Options. The purpose of this chapter is to provide the reader with some in-depth insights about methods which may best be utilized to arouse and maintain the interest component by properly developing the Learning Activity Option portion of Individual Study Units.

FUNCTION OF LEARNING ACTIVITY OPTIONS

In order to provide a means whereby the instructional program can meet the varied needs, interests and abilities of each student, well-designed Learning Activity Options are employed in the Individual Study Units to facilitate learning in the following ways:

1. To generate and maintain interest, as well as to motivate the student so that once the student is exposed to the Learning Experience, his "learning opportunities" have been nurtured and he is well on his way to a full course of knowledge.
2. Relevance is introduced through related life experiences so that the student is eager to learn.
3. Human variables in behavior and attitudes are met through a multitude of different methods and techniques for learning.
4. The student has a voice in what he is to learn and how he is to learn it, which provides him with maximum opportunities for involvement.
5. The student becomes responsible for most of his learning, and therefore, he is more apt to learn.

DEVELOPING LEARNING ACTIVITY OPTIONS

There are numerous methods and techniques which can be employed to enable a youngster to learn. One contemporary approach to education is to provide the youngster with several options to choose from in determining how he is going to proceed on his learning journey. When formulating Learning Activity Options, there are four points which must be considered:

1. The instructions must be explicit in delineating what the student is to do. If certain options are required, then they should be so designated. No more than 40 percent of the total number of options should be required for initial completion by the student, so that in case he is to be re-cycled through the Unit at some future time there will be ample Learning Activity Options for him to complete the second time around. In all cases, the student should be instructed to check off those options which he selects for completion.
2. The options should be written on several different reading levels.
3. The options should be developed so that they will serve as an aid to the student in reaching the stated Behavioral Objectives.
4. There should be a variety of options, including reading assignments, and learning through acting, writing, listening and observing.

The following are recommended for the development of Learning

Activity Options. Each option may be dealt with in a number of different ways. Most of the suggested individual options can be broken down in at least ten or twenty different ways. Many of the options may be developed progressively toward another option. If a progressive option is employed, then the initial option required for completion by the student to start the chain of progress must be designated.

Acquiring Knowledge Through Action (Doing)

1. Simulate a Real Life Experience

By simulating a real life experience, the student actually places himself in the role of the person involved in a particular situation. The student might be asked to play the role of the mayor of the community, an astronaut on the way to the moon, a teacher in a classroom, or the President of the United States. Once the student has been instructed to assume a role, he is then presented with a particular situation to determine how he, in the role, would respond to one or more problems.

2. Visit and Take Part in a Real Life Situation

This option can provide a student with the opportunity to be involved in history-making or occupationally predictive events. For example, the student might travel with a newspaper reporter to eyewitness certain events; he might visit an excavation site to learn how a building or bridge is built; or he might volunteer to do some work with a social agency. There are a number of situations like these which come readily to mind. Of course, after the student's participation in a real life situation, he should be required to make either an oral or written presentation, or complete a test designed to examine the quantity and quality of his learning in the particular learning venture.

3. Perform Some Type of Exploration

Students selecting this option might be asked to explore some location which is pertinent to the subject area under study. This might include an exploration of the dumps, visiting a community, exploring the remains of some ruins, or a host of other situations which demand exploration. The student might also explore maps, charts and graphs, etc.

4. Perform Some Experiment

Students might be required in the Learning Activity Options to conduct certain experiments and observe the results. It should not be assumed that this option is confined to the study of science, for it can present viable opportunities to learn in the subject areas of mathematics, social science, and almost any other area of interest. For example, if the teacher wishes a student to discover how a message is changed as it is transmitted from person to person, she might direct the student to recite a message to a designated person who would then re-route it to another person. The performance might be repeated down a row of ten students. The student would then check to see how the content of the message had been changed as well as the interpretation which the last student had received before he gave his teacher an explanation for changes in the verbal transmittal of a message. Another experiment might consist of having a student place himself about three paces from a wall before bending his trunk towards the wall until he is positioned at an approximate 90 degree angle. He should then be instructed to try to pick up a chair which has been placed immediately beneath him and then attempt to rise. Continuing with the experiment the student would be directed to ask a female student to duplicate the experiment. The student would then be called upon to explain the difference in the results while providing supportive elaboration on the cause of the difference.

5. Conduct a Survey

This option is one which is usually well received by students at the secondary level. However, students at the lower levels are by no means precluded from selecting this option for they, too, are well able to carry out such an assignment. The student may be required to choose a subject or problem which he feels should be investigated within the community. He might then be committed to devising a questionnaire survey format to obtain and record the reactions of the subjects he chooses for his sampling. This survey should, of course, include some of the school population, as well as have content which relates to some subject under study in the school curriculum.

6. Take Photographs

This particular option is usually well received by students. No doubt this can be attributed to the fact that students are permitted to take photographs of any subject which interests them provided that it revolves around or can be integrated into a particular subject area. When the photographs have been taken, the student may be required to put "captions" under the photos. Another appealing project might entail the preparation by the student of a "picture book." There are a number of different assignments which may be given to the student who selects this option.

7. Go on an Excursion for the Purpose of Acquiring Information

An option which might be stimulating to some students would involve taking an excursion to a particular place of interest in order to obtain different kinds of information. There is a wide range of sites to choose from and these might include the post office, the public library, the museum, the police station, the fire house, another school, a shopping center, etc. However, taking an excursion means getting parental permission and may well involve some expense, so this option should be well prepared in advance.

8. Create an Exhibit

This option, while it does have certain limitations, may be used to stimulate a group of students pursuing the same unit of study to arrange for an exhibit of some of the work which they have prepared. This option can be undertaken in almost any area, including science, social studies, language arts, mathematics, etc. In fact, the teacher should try to incorporate this option into all areas, as often as possible, because it does serve as a motivating device.

9. Undertake Role Playing to Enact Problems, Events and Concerns

The student or students who select this option may be given a problem to dramatize by role playing. For example, to simulate the interviewing process, one student might role-play the employer while another student may assume the role of a teacher presenting a lesson to the class. One creative teacher devised a role-playing option in which the student assumed the role of the mayor of the community and interviewed several community citizens to ascertain their views of the most pressing problems in the community.

10. Make a Film

Students will enjoy making a film. This option might be completed in almost any given subject area. To perform this task, a number of students must opt for this activity to form a team of individual members assigned to different functions. For example, a student-writer will be responsible for creating a suitable script. Perhaps two or more may be necessary, each of them working in unison on various sections of the film. If film scripts are going to be written, then one or several student-photographers will be responsible for taking pictures. If an 8 mm or a 16 mm camera is going to be used, then one or several student-cameramen will be needed. Someone who is proficient in art work may be needed to offer guidance to student-artists engaged in making scenarios, signs, etc. Several student-engineers may also be needed to tape various portions of the film. A student crew of lighting "experts," technicians, make-up artists, carpenters, and many other assistants may be necessary which will provide maximum opportunities for involvement by a host of youngsters participating in the experience of film-making.

11. Collect Descriptions, Reports, Interviews and Responses to Questions

This option might require the student to collect materials which would aid in the educational process. The fact that he has to collect the information and use the Thought Process of Translation certainly will enable him to learn about the Unit. The student might be required to write a brief report to be distributed to other students relaying information obtained from reports and interviews.

12. Build Scale Models and Drawings

Because of the extensive amount of time which this option might entail, it should be utilized sparingly. A group of students might be required to build a scale model of the Shakespearean stage, or individual students might design and plan illustrations for the script of a dramatic presentation in which the students wish to be involved. This particular option has demonstrated effectiveness in English, Mechanical Drawing, and Industrial Arts; however, it obviously can, with some ingenuity, be employed in other areas.

13. Hold a Group Discussion

Students who select this option might be grouped by interest and asked to discuss a common topic. The option might direct the group to select a chairman and a recorder. The chairman would keep the discussion from becoming disorderly and the recorder would be responsible for maintaining a summary of the discussion.

14. Use of Educational Games

This particular option has far-reaching educational implications. Part of this may be attributed to the fact that more and more of the large educational publishing firms are allotting vast sums of money to the production of educational games for the market. Many of these games utilize the technique of role playing in order that the student can assimilate certain conditions which exist. One such game is the Manchester Empire published by the Educational Development Corporation, Brattle Square, Cambridge, Massachusetts. Some creative teachers have also developed their own games to help reinforce learning in their subject area. There seems to be little doubt that most progressive schools of the future will make extensive use of educational games to enhance learning.

15. Use Community and Governmental Resources

To complete this option, the student might be required to visit a number of community and governmental resources to obtain information pertinent to the subject area he is studying. These might include the local post office, courthouse, police station, fire house, Internal Revenue Service, etc. Long range plans might include a trip to some fairly distant place such as the Federal or State capitols to visit the offices of government located there.

Acquiring Knowledge Through Writing

1. Write Short Stories, Articles, Speeches

Students who select this option are given the opportunity to exercise their literary skills by developing a short story, an article, speech or other literary production which displays their writing talents. As a part of this option, the student should also be required to tape the short story or speech. In addition, a better evaluation of the student's talent might be made were the student required to deliver the speech before an audience of his peers.

2. Write Letters, Thank You Notes

This option might require a student, who had previously chosen an option of interviewing a noted personage, to write a "Thank You" letter expressing appreciation for the person's cooperation. Teachers have been using this teaching technique for years, and it should continue to be a favorite of students.

3. Prepare an Agenda for a Meeting

This option may also be progressively geared to dovetail and lead into another option. The student may be requested to prepare an agenda for a meeting with a noted person over the Speakerphone, an agenda for a field trip, or an agenda for a Parent-Teacher meeting. There are a number of varied meetings for which a suitable agenda might be suggested and devised by students to eventually serve as teaching-learning devices.

4. Write Scripts for Plays, Operas, Radio or Television Dramas

This option has limitless possibilities. Students who have selected the option might be required to meet as a group and decide on a script for either of the dramatic presentations mentioned. Various members of the group might then be delegated the task of preparing different portions or sections of the script. An obvious adjunctive option would be the arrangements for dramatization and live presentation of the script.

5. Prepare Radio and Television Programs

In this option, the student would be asked to prepare a program which is pertinent to a unit of study and might be televised or broadcast. Students are fascinated by hearing their voices and seeing themselves; therefore, the wise teacher should capitalize on this by insisting that the students produce quality work which might be broadcast or televised.

6. Prepare a Lesson to Be Given to a Group in Class

One of the best methods by which a student may learn a particular lesson is the activity of learning by teaching. The student would prepare himself to teach a lesson to another class of younger children, or to instruct a large body of students on a subject with which he is thoroughly familiar and therefore is well equipped to teach. This student would first be required to prepare an outline of his lesson to be submitted to the instructor for initial approval. When he has received this approval, he would next write out the content of the entire lesson to be presented. The student might also be responsible for devising an examination to be administered after he has presented the lesson. The development of a school program of "student teaching-learning" which would involve a group of several students being responsible for teaching a number of sessions might also be a very meaningful option in this category.

7. List Questions of Interest for Individual and Group Use

This option permits the student to use his Thought Process of Evaluation to list questions of interest which should be pursued in order to gain relevant information about a certain subject or topic. In this option, the student might list his own questions to serve as an evaluation of his progress through the Unit. A number of students participating in a group might list questions which they themselves should be able to answer if they are going to learn the Unit.

8. Prepare an Outline for Individual Activities

In this option, the student might be required to prepare an outline for an educational activity dealing with attitudes. This kind of progressive option would serve to lead into another option capable of providing substance in the Unit and reinforcing learning.

9. Prepare Programs for Sharing with Others

Students selecting this option might be required to develop some program pertinent to a particular unit of studies which could then be shared with other students. Such a program could very well be a public relations program for the school, a progress report program for parents, or a host of other programs either about the school or events in the community.

10. Develop a Plan or Scheme

Here, a student might be required to devise a plan or schema for accomplishing some activity. This might involve developing an improved plan for exiting from school buildings in the event of fire, a schema for the operation of some educational machine, a plan for classroom management, a plan for cleaning up the classroom, a plan for keeping notes, or a plan for helping others. There are numerous ways in which this option might be developed for reinforcing learning.

11. Prepare Maps, Charts, Tables or Diagrams

In order to reinforce learning, a required option might very well be for the student to devise a map, a chart, tables, or a diagram pertinent to the Individual Study Unit. This option might also be used as a means of determining how well the student comprehends the Unit.

Acquiring Knowledge Through Reading

1. Read a Book, Magazine or Newspaper Article, Reference or Supplementary Reading Materials.

This will probably be the most widely used option of all. Students may be directed to read any materials, from the labels on cans of foodstuffs to certain features of the *Wall Street Journal.* The teacher must be thoroughly cognizant of the student's reading ability when making such assignments to insure that the suggested materials are not too difficult for the student's comprehension. One technique which has been used successfully by a creative teacher is to require a student to read a short story and then rewrite the theme of the story, substituting the student's community and his friends as the main characters. A student might also be asked to do comparative research by reading an article on the same subject reported on by the three most commonly read local newspapers; or he might be asked to isolate an article which was not reported on in one of the newspapers and prepare his own written "report" of it for that newspaper. A student might also be asked to do research reading from several sources in the library or instructional materials center to secure documentation for a report he is required to submit under a preceding option.

2. Do Research in the Library

This option may be used for any subject area, and the learning activity might involve a search by the student for some information pertinent to his area of interest in a library or instructional materials center. This option will not only serve as an aid for the student in learning how to use the library or instructional materials center more effectively, but it will also give him confidence when other occasions arise where it is necessary for him to research other information. A student might be asked to determine the number of students attending elementary public schools in the community and in the state for the 1969 school year. However, at no time should the teacher give directions to the student as to the particular reference work which would most likely have the information he is seeking. A very important aspect of this option is the resourcefulness which the student is called upon to utilize in obtaining the information sought.

Acquiring Knowledge Through Listening and Observing

1. Contact a Noted Personage on the Speakerphone

This technique, which is highly contemporary in character, has been extremely useful in contacting various persons for a conversation where it has been, in the past, well nigh impossible to reach such persons. When this option is included as a choice, prior arrangements should have already been made. A prior appointment with the "noted personage" may be made either by telephone or written correspondence. This option may involve some expense, depending upon where the call is directed. Therefore, it is economically feasible to make provision for a number of students to participate in the interview rather than restricting it to a single student.

2. Visit a School, Museum, Municipal Building or Art Gallery

This option offers the student an opportunity to visit a school, museum, municipal building, art gallery, or any place where he can ascertain information relevant to his studies. More and more schools are making better use of these resources to provide better and more varied educational opportunities for students. In Philadelphia, Pennsylvania, the Philadelphia School District has initiated an educational program in which students attend a number of "outside school" educational facilities to continue their education, such as museums, newspaper offices, etc. By special arrangements, students may prevail upon the authorities for the use of these public facilities for a period of several days rather than several hours. These "outside school" education ventures have been found to be generally attractive to students.

3. Attend a Conference, Forum or Seminar

This option will permit a student or several students to attend some event which is pertinent to a particular Individual Study Unit. The student or students might be required to report the salient parts either to a group of interested students, parents or to the teacher. Since this option may include some expense for transportation and incidental costs, it should be planned well in advance. A possible assignment within this option might be taping the discussion and subsequently writing a brief report to be distributed to the class or the entire school population.

4. See a Play, Musical or Opera

This option provides the youngsters with an opportunity to view a play, musical or opera which should be related to something which is being studied in school. For example, if *Hamlet* is the subject under study, this option would certainly enhance learning if the student found it possible to attend the theatre and see this or another Shakespearean play. This option will require additional cost to the students and may be difficult to implement in a poor community.

5. View a Television Program, a 16 mm Film, or a Movie Mover

This option requires the student to view television or a 16 mm film before completing a test or preparing a report on what he has seen. The Movie Mover has met with much success in a number of schools throughout the country, because it provides maximum utilization of costly 16 mm film and projectors which were previously stored in a "visual aids room" for 90 percent of the time. With the use of the Movie Mover, 16 mm projectors can be operated to allow a single student to see and hear without disturbing other classmates in the same room.

6. Interview a Resource Person for Information

This option requires that the student interview someone to obtain information, and presents a wide range for choice. The student might interview a doctor to get information on narcotics; he might visit the office of an accountant to learn something about depreciation; or he might visit an insurance broker for information about the different types, purposes and costs of various insurance policies. In addition, the County Clerk is an invaluable source to go to for information about the student's community. This option offers an unlimited range of possibilities upon which the creative and imaginative teacher can build.

7. Visit a Television or Radio Station

This option may require a visit by the student to a television or radio broadcasting studio to observe a program which is pertinent to a lesson under study. He may also be required to participate in the program to some extent if such arrangements can be made in advance with the broadcasting company.

8. Utilize the Tools of Educational Technology

This option has unlimited use. There are literally hundreds of educational machines which do hosts of things both intricate and simple, such as responding to a human command or reacting to an incorrect response. An individualized instructional program cannot possibly survive without the use of some educational technology. A major point of concern, however, is that there be a variety of machines and equipment to enhance the learning program and to afford students the choice of a multitude of different methods and techniques to learn. At the elementary level, the Language Master has been used quite successfully, while the Auto-Tutor has met with success at the secondary level. These are only two of the vast number of machines which have achieved good results. When the teacher is constructing an option for the use of educational technology, he should make certain that all instructions are very clear as to what machines to use, what accoutrements, such as tape or film, are to be utilized in the machine, and where the machine and these materials are located. The major advantage of the educational machines lies in their versatility, for they can be used to teach, instruct, test or help the student to evaluate his own program.

9. Utilize the Learning Center or a Laboratory

Most modern and progressive schools have made provisions in the physical plant for learning centers and laboratories. Where this is the case, students may be directed to these places to receive instructions or make observations of a specialized nature.

SUMMARY

Learning Activity Options are an essential and important part of any individualized instructional program. Appropriately developed options will generate and maintain interest, introduce relevancy, provide consideration of human variables, enable the student to have a voice in what and how he will learn, as well as permit him to assume some responsibility for most of his learning. The activities which a student may engage in through the selection of Learning Activity Options may be broken down into four categories:

1. Acquisition of knowledge through action;
2. Acquisition of knowledge through writing;
3. Acquisition of knowledge through reading;
4. Acquisition of knowledge through listening and observing.

Since the major responsibility of the educator is to reinforce learning, it may be said that the Learning Activity Options are the core of an individualized instructional program.

9

Developing
Attitudinal Objectives

For years, teachers have assumed the acquisition of certain attitudes by students. Part of this may be partially due to the "intangible substance" of attitudes which, unlike behavior, are difficult to evaluate in terms of observable competence and performance. It may also be that educators feel that if they simply concentrate on obtaining certain behavioral responses, desirable attitudes would be simultaneously produced. Some importance may be attached to the fact that autocratic teachers of yesteryear failed to fully understand the significance of attitude in terms of how it affects behavior. Today, however, it is apparent that the area of attitudes is one which has been too long neglected in education. This is quite obvious when we examine newspapers and magazines, and view our television screens, to be confronted with the results of certain attitudes across the country which are supporting a revolutionary quest for change. Changes are being sought both in students' traditional attitudes as well as their traditional behavior. A most lucid example of this is the fierce struggle of black people inspired by self-pride and a desire for greater respect of the black image.

If learning were simply a response to a stimulus without any external or internal factors which tangentially affected it, then the educator's task would be much easier. However, as we read in Chapter 5 on Identifying Behavioral Objectives, there are several factors which affect learning, such as the characteristics of the learner, association, motivation and reinforcement. Therefore, taking these factors into consideration, the educator's real responsibility is to induce, improve and encourage learning. In fulfilling this responsibility, an additional area which must be isolated and considered is attitude. With reference to this, an educator's primary focus would be on changing or re-orienting attitudes so that they will exert a favorable rather than a detrimental influence on learning.

SOME COMPONENTS OF ATTITUDE

The human being is a complex organism comprised of a multitude of complementary components which enmesh to produce human attitudes. These components are:

1. *Intellectual Areas* which gather, store and process information, ideas and values;
2. *Emotional Areas* which are molded by experiences, family, friends and group membership;
3. *Cognitive Areas* which consist of movements or impulses to make or take a stand for or against something.

The foregoing attempt to define component parts or areas which produce human attitude is not completely justifiable for everyone, but they might be more generally described as emotionally toned learned or acquired tendencies to respond positively or negatively, favorably or unfavorably, to persons, groups, objects, situations, ideas, or events.

THE SOURCES OF ATTITUDE

The sources of attitudes are very complex. Attitudes can be nurtured in or arise out of contacts with parents, teachers, the community or the environment in which the student has lived. We realize that learning is going on although a learner may be unaware that he is learning, and the person identified with such learning may have no intention of teaching or producing learning in the unaware recipient.

Primary responsibility to teach "correct" attitudes rests with the schools and parents. What "correct" attitudes are is difficult to say and they often vary with individual considerations. Perhaps the only viable method for identifying correct attitudes is to describe them as those attitudes which should be developed in order to produce the desired behavior educators seek to produce by the presentation of facts, generalizations, concepts and ideas. The reader must bear in mind that attitudes are only partly intellectual in nature, and that they are also emotionally saturated. Because of this, unlearning or changing attitudes will be extremely difficult. This is one reason why traditionalism has been very difficult to remove from the activities and attitudes of educators. For years, educators have experienced and practiced behavior which resulted in the inculcation of a "narrow" approach to education which insidiously infected teacher's minds.

The reader may ask: "How can correct attitudes be taught as a subject area such as, for example, history or mathematics?" Although the idea seems foreign to many educators, this author believes that this is possible, however, providing only that the instructor understands that correct attitudes will always be relatively individualistic in nature and the "correct" attitudinal response may consequently be difficult to evoke. For example, a person who has not been exposed to the same conditions, experiences, environment and persons may exhibit an attitudinal response essentially different from a person who is familiar with diametrically opposed situations. An excellent example of this is the fact that many black authors believe that only a black person who has been raised in a certain environment can adequately portray certain attitudes of the black man. By utilizing Individual Study Units, an attempt is made not primarily to change a student's attitude from "x" to "y," but to provide him with sufficient experience to broaden his perceptions and viewpoint so that he may be more prone to arrive at "desirable" attitudes. The dialogue which may or may not occur at the attitude section of the Individual Study Unit is primarily for the teacher and student to exchange ideas so that the student may acquire additional facts and insights to justify, change or re-orient his acquired attitudes. The reader should be cognizant of the fact that there is no single "correct" attitudinal response for each and every person, but that each individual's attitude must be considered, analyzed and elaborated upon in the context of the whole fabric of that individual's personality formation according to his environment and his life conditions.

FIVE LEVELS OF ATTITUDINAL ATTAINMENT

The development of human attitudes is generally a gradual and ongoing process. An attitude which may begin with a single, instantaneous bolt of awareness may develop into an important part of the student's character and personality. The following discussion of the five levels of human attitude attainment is based on a classification system developed by David R. Krathwohl, Benjamin S. Bloom, and Bertram B. Masia: [1]

1. *Receiving:* This is the lowest level of attitude attainment. At this level, the student is aware of the existence of certain phenomena and stimuli, such as a

[1] Krathwohl, David R., Bloom, Benjamin S., Masia, Bertram B., *Taxonomy of Educational Objectives, Handbook II: Affective Domain* (New York: David McKay, Inc. 1964).

situation, an idea, or an object, and the student is willing to give it some attention or to receive it.

Examples: Awareness—The student recognizes the importance of the subject agreeing with the verb.

Willingness to Receive—The student listens to the teacher explaining a prepositional phrase.

Concentrated or Selective Attention—The student has a preference for reading the literary works of Morton Thompson.

2. *Responding:* At this level, the student is merely interested in the situation, idea, object, or other phenomena. He desires to learn more about it and gets a degree of satisfaction from working on it and investigating it.

Examples: Acquiescence in Responding—The student is willing to complete his homework on capitalization and punctuation.

Willingness to Respond—The student voluntarily reads books and magazines to improve his vocabulary.

Satisfaction in Response—The student reads the book entitled *Nat Turner* by William Styron for personal pleasure.

3. *Believing:* At this level of attitude attainment, the student believes that a situation, idea, object, or other phenomena has definite worth and that it is better than any other alternative. He demonstrates consistent belief to the extent that others are aware of his belief. He may even try to get others to become committed to his belief.

Examples: Acceptance of a Value—The student internalizes an appreciation of Shakespeare.

Preference for a Value—The student assumes an active role in establishing an Afro-American Resource Center.

Commitment—The student is actively involved in getting school officials to implement Linguistic English into the school program.

4. *Organization:* The student relates his newly acquired attitudes to other attitudes he already possesses. He may do this by either modifying or adding to his previously developed attitudes. The degrees in which the attitude component of organization may be evidenced in a student are:
A. Conceptualization of a Value
Example: The student attempts to identify the characteristics of Walt Whitman's writing which he admires.

B. Organization of a Value System
Example: The student begins to form judgments as to the thrust in which Linguistic English is moving in American schools.

5. *Characterization:* For the student this is the highest level of attitude attainment. At this level, his belief has become so much a part of his total person that it is characteristic of his personality and total outlook on life.
Generalized
A. The student has confidence in his ability to write logical and clear sentences.

B. Characteristics—The student develops an unconscious attitude which is readily identifiable.

METHODS FOR REALIZING ATTITUDES

The last assignment of every Individual Study Unit should be concerned with the constructive development of attitudes through first-hand experiences, or through reasoned evidence and logic. In order to permit attitudinal development, there are basically three instructional plans for the student:

1. Examination-Question Plan

Through adequate evaluation, which should include written responses and/or general observations, attitude can be developed and examined.

Example: Do you think it matters very much for ghetto children to learn the various parts of a sentence?

2. Goals and Objectives Plan

In this plan, preferred attitudes are realized through the medium of educational objectives. The objectives should consist of two ingredients, or components:

A. The condition must be stated, indicating what will be used to help create, reinforce, re-orient or change the desired attitude.

B. The attitude attainment must be stated using appropriate terminology such as willingness, desire, faith, belief, appreciation, realization, open mindedness, feeling. (Refer to Figure 9-1 for additional terms.)

Example: You will be able to write a critical review indicating your own point of view.

3. Learning Experience Plan

This plan helps to realize attitudes by presenting certain experiences which will manifest certain "desirable" attitudes in the students. The experiences so indicated should "arouse" attitudes which are appropriate for aiding the development of the Behavioral Objectives.

Example: If one were to ask several different people who Langston Hughes was, a multitude of responses might be given—He was an American; he was a black man; he was a novelist; he was a poet; he was a philosopher; he was a world traveler, etc. In order for us to come to our own conclusion as to what Langston Hughes was, we will have to read several of his works and attempt to analyze why he wrote as he did; what

AFFECTIVE DOMAIN

RECEIVE	RESPONSE	VALUE	ORGANIZATION	CHARACTERIZATION
Understand Comprehend Learn Apprehend Perceive Grasp Follow	Acknowledge Echo Amenable Selects Chooses Participates Gathers Visits Argues	Faith Trust Belief Confidence Reliance Trustworthy Dependable Put One's Trust in Place Reliance on Swear by Rely upon Supports Subscribes	Systematize Arrange Classify Coordinate Establish Correlate Methodize	Type Representative Subjectiveness Typify Identify

FIGURE 9-1.

LEVELS OF ATTITUDE ATTAINMENT AND THEIR IDENTIFIABLE TERMS

thoughts he was trying to convey; the extent to which these thoughts were influenced by his varied experiences as a man, as a traveler, as an American and as a member of a racial minority.

When each of us has completed the learning activity options, we may each have a different belief about the creativity of Langston Hughes; a different feeling about certain of his poems and short stories; and a different hope or expectation for writers with similar styles who seek to achieve success. Our primary purpose will be to discover how our personal attitudes have been reinforced, changed or modified after reading several selections by Langston Hughes.

CLASSIFICATION OF ATTITUDES

Some attitudes should be developed by the school program, and some should not. Those attitudes falling into the latter category generally involve religious beliefs, particularly those dealing with the existence of an omnipotent being. However, the following general ideas are fit subjects of attitudes in which a school program should seek to involve itself:

1. Attitudes Toward Acquisition of Knowledge

If a student comes into a classroom with a preconceived attitude about learning, then this internalized impediment or obstruction must first be removed by the instructor before any learning can take place. Many students have had experiences with failure which lead them to believe that they will not be able to competently manage learning so they withdraw and reject the intrusion of knowledge. Many students have had long experiences with the boredom which comes from continued presentation of irrelevant or incomprehensible material, so they close the shutters of their minds to the acquisition of any more such "knowledge."

2. Attitudes Toward One's Reason

Many students come to school with a much reduced concept of their problem-solving capabilities. Much of this comes from repeated experiences with failure and the absence of opportunities to excel. Consequently, such students have no faith in their ability to absorb, recodify, translate and apply knowledge and feel threatened when materials are presented to them because they are afraid that if they acquire knowledge they will be expected to utilize it in some way and they have no faith in their ability to do so.

3. Attitudes Toward Others and Their Culture

During the early stages of a child's socialization by his parents, he acquires and adopts certain attitudes which they exhibit toward other peoples and other cultures. His parents' likes and dislikes are the only examples a child has to follow for a long period of time when he is learning the best ways of coping with his environment. Consequently, many children have internalized prejudicial and unsupported attitudes held by their parents without ever subjecting such attitudes to tests of fact. Therefore, when information is presented which is directly opposite to the attitude the student has internalized the student tends to reject it, questions not only what he believes is his own innate belief, but what is actually an acquired belief; as well as the veracity of those parents from whom he has acquired the belief.

4. Attitudes Toward the World

These attitudes, too, come partially from the same source as those in "3" above, with important additional factors. These attitudes are usually the result of the child's early experiences with other people besides his parents, the world of imagery which the child is exposed to by books, television, plays, etc., as well as those attitudes which the child forms through the use of his own imagination and reasoning processes. Attitudes such as these, which may be sometimes partially correct and partially incorrect, can hinder the acquisition of knowledge by coloring it or making it seem irrational because of the student's inability to reconcile diverse elements in the material to be learned, some of which agree with his precognitions and some of which are diametrically opposed.

5. Attitudes Toward One's Self and Being

Many children have internalized poor self-images about themselves and their immense value as a human being. These children are so confused psychologically and emotionally that it is extremely difficult for them to acquire knowledge about materials presented to them until their own inner turmoil has been resolved.

SUMMARY

The attitudes a student carries with him will have an effect on his ability to learn. Therefore, no longer can schools neglect this highly important area. Although much research is needed in this area, some consideration should be given to teaching attitudes also when English or Mathematics is taught in school. Basically, there are three components to the total attitude.

The intellectual area gathers, stores and processes information, ideas and values. The emotional area, which is biologically oriented, is molded by experience, friends, family and other groups. The cognitive area controls impulses or movements in support of or against something. There are several basic sources of attitude formation, most of which deal with people and the environment. There are five levels of attitude attainment which rest on an ascending scale from lowest to highest, as follows:

1. Receiving takes place when the student becomes aware of the existence of something or someone.
2. Response takes place when the student is merely interested in something or someone.
3. Believing occurs when the student has concluded that something or someone has definite worth.
4. Organization takes place when the student relates and integrates newly-acquired attitudes with those which he already possesses.
5. Characterization, the highest level of attitude attainment, takes place when the attitude becomes a total part of the person's personality.

The three methods which may be used for examining and realizing attitudes are (1) examination questions; (2) goals and objectives; and (3) learning experiences. Attitudes may be classified in five basic areas where they control or influence reactions which affect the educational process:

1. Attitudes toward the acquisition of knowledge;
2. Attitudes toward one's reason;
3. Attitudes toward others and their culture;
4. Attitudes toward the world; and
5. Attitudes toward one's self and being.

It is extremely difficult to evaluate attitudes because the teacher may unconsciously infect the student with his own "hang-up." Perhaps the greatest value in concerning ourselves with Attitudinal Objectives is the opportunity it allows us of providing the student with a much broader perspective upon which he can base his own attitudes.

10

Evaluating the Individualized
Instructional Program

Evaluation is an essential, an integral, and an ongoing part of the teaching-learning process as it relates to the utilization of Individual Study Units. It enables the students and teachers to know how much progress has been made and what can be done to improve performance. Evaluation also helps the teacher to judge the effectiveness of the Individual Study Unit and will reveal the strengths and weaknesses of the Unit. It is in this section of the Individual Study Unit that the changing role of the teacher is clearly delineated because, in this single section, he assumes a multiplicity of roles:

1. That of a resource person who can direct students to additional materials and equipment to enhance the learning experience for the student;
2. That of a guidance counselor who can provide guidance and counseling to the student throughout the learning experience;
3. That of a psychologist who is able to confer with and gain insights about the student's attitudinal response prior to prescribing curative guidance and direction;
4. That of a generalist who is able to aid the student in varied learning opportunities which occur from day to day. Sometimes the generalist will don the role of a mother, a father, or even a big brother or sister and, whenever a crisis arises, will aid in the behavioral and attitudinal development of the student.

Basic Principles of Evaluation

Evaluation, as we have previously learned, is an essential part of education. There are several basic principles underlying any evaluation program. These are:

1. It should indicate student growth in terms of the Thought Processes and Derivatives, Attitudinal Objectives and Psycho-Motor Skills. At all times, evaluation should indicate the progress being made toward the achievement of Behavioral Objectives as they relate to the Thought Processes and Derivatives. It should also include provision for the examination of attitude and, possibly, for development of Psycho-Motor skills.

2. It should be closely related to the Behavioral Objectives of the student and teacher. In addition, evaluation should indicate the degree to which the student has been successful in meeting specific goals as outlined in the Behavioral Objectives. It should also indicate whether or not other goals should be sought.

3. It should be a continuous process. No teacher should wait until the end of the Individual Study Unit to evaluate the progress of the student. It should be administered periodically in stages to check progress as the student pursues his learning experience, constituting a checkpoint where, if necessary, additional directions and recommendations may be made.

4. It should be initiated by the use of several strategies to assess student educational growth. A well-rounded and carefully planned evaluation program includes a multitude of evaluative strategies such as the following:

   a. Observing students while they are working to look for boredom, disinterest or frustration. These are early signs which may clue the teacher to the student who may find his assignment too difficult, or may not understand what is expected of him.

   b. Try out a few checkpoint questions from either the Self-Test or Pre-Test.

   c. Confer with the student to carefully probe the extent of his growth.

   d. Collect and examine some of the materials the student has been working on to check his growth.

   e. Confer with any assistants who may be serving as aides to the teacher about the student.

   A point of concern here is that no single evaluation strategy should be considered "best," but all or one should be used at the discretion of the teacher in terms of the individual student who is the subject of the evaluation. However, because of the time a teacher must and should spend working with individual students, the evaluation strategy should not be too time-consuming. If it is at all possible, para-professionals should be employed to assist the teacher in *marking* only, bearing in mind, however, that it is the teacher's task to make a reasoned evaluation from the grades indicated by the para-professional.

5. The results of the evaluation should be so indicated on the Unit and other records. In any effective individualized program, keeping accurate and careful records is mandatory. Whenever notations as to the progress of the student are made on the Unit, the date of the observation or checkpoint should also be indicated.

6. Students should also be encouraged to evaluate their own progress. As schools become more and more interested in the individualization of instruction, the student will assume an ever-increasing role in his education. One of the student's new roles will be that of evaluator of his own progress. In certain cases, the student will also be permitted to prescribe his next Unit. When individualized instruction is really on the move, students should be permitted to develop and complete their own Unit for study. There are many ways in which students can become involved in their evaluation. However, four of the most basic ways are listed below:

   a. *Individual Evaluation*—Before the student proceeds through the Individual Study Unit after reading the Behavioral Objectives, he could establish some sub-objectives as yardsticks for measuring his own progress.

   b. *Group Evaluation*—Students who have selected identical options may confer in small groups to determine whether they have reached the stated Behavioral Objectives. If the members of the group learn that there is some variation in the response, then a short discussion should follow to find the course so that those students who are "off the track" may get "back on the track."

   c. *Teacher-Pupil Evaluation*—The teacher, by holding individual conferences with students, can evaluate academic progress. From this, he can also provide direction for the student to continue his learning experience.

   d. *Team Learning Evaluation*—In a team learning situation where two or three students meet to discuss and evaluate a common learning activity option, progress may be effectively evaluated.

Evaluation of the Cognitive Domain

The cognitive domain involves the Thought Processes. Since thought involves thinking and thinking is a process of the mind, it is therefore not directly observable. However, the teacher can evaluate a student's growth in terms of the Thought Processes by observing the student's involvement in situations and experiences. The reader must bear in mind that each student, regardless of his abilities, should be offered opportunities to develop all of the Thought Processes and Thought Derivatives as they pertain to the Unit under study. The Behavioral Objectives and the Attitudinal Objectives are the guidelines on which tests should be constructed so that the Individual Study Unit may be adequately evaluated. The reader must be cautioned that the important components of the Individual Study Units, such as Behavioral Objectives, Learning Experience and Learning Activity Options, do not primarily involve only the lowest Thought Process, i.e., Remembering. For example, the question: "Name and describe the parts of speech in your own words," would involve the higher level Thought Process of Translating.

Evaluation in the Cognitive Domain also involves the student's ability to use facts, concepts and generalizations which have been acquired in the learning experience, and how well he can apply this knowledge to new situations. Therefore, it is necessary to evaluate how well students think.

The teacher may observe his students in action as they pursue their learning options. Some students will try to select non-problem solving options, while others will not. It is up to the teacher to re-direct the students from time to time, so that all students get their share of problem-solving options.

When students select identical options and are grouped for small group instruction, the teacher can evaluate student progress and performance as it relates to understanding the option under consideration. An excellent technique for evaluating group discussion is by taping the discussion and making it available later to play back for further discussion by the student.

Evaluation of the Affective Domain

The development of constructive attitudes is most difficult to evaluate insofar as learning is concerned. It is difficult to determine what a student really feels or believes because he is often not sure of his own feelings and opinions. It is also quite possible that when the student is examined about his feelings he may give answers which he thinks the teacher wants while, in reality, the student does not feel that way at all. In addition, as brought out in Chapter 9, teachers have their own "hang-ups" and these may interfere with their objective evaluations. However, the affective domain is much too important to leave to chance. If education is going to permit students to take their rightful place in society, one of the responsibilities of the school is to lead the development of constructive attitudes.

Basically, there are several techniques which can be used in evaluating attitudes. However, these techniques may be grouped into two categories, i.e.:

1. Observation
2. Asking questions

Observation: Observation is probably the best method of evaluating pupil attitudes. Students usually reveal a great deal about themselves as they discuss situations and problems with their peers, and perform in group situations. Therefore, by observing them in action, the teacher can also discover many things about the student.

Asking Questions: Asking questions of students, either verbal or written, may provide the teacher with information pertaining to the student's interest, feeling and belief. Examination questions may be given to the student in a number of techniques, such as:

1. Present statement that expresses opinions, feelings, or beliefs. Ask students to present their views pro or con.
2. Ask students what they enjoyed or disliked about an event.
3. Ask students to reply to questions such as "Do you believe. . . ?" "Why or why not. . . ?" "What do you think. . . ?"
4. Present students with unfinished statements directing them to complete the statement in their own words.

Evaluating Behavioral Objectives

The major purpose for seeking an evaluation of Behavioral Objectives is to pinpoint the classification of knowledge toward which the student is to direct his Learning Activities and to determine the Thought Processes to be realized. Only in this way can we assess the value of the knowledge as it pertains to the student behavior and be able to adequately construct test questions appropriate to the Behavioral Objective. The chart illustrated in Figure 10-1 is a useful tool for evaluation. To clarify its use, let us refer to a Behavioral Objective contained in a student's Individual Study Unit.

Behavioral Objective:

Given this unit on the study of prepositional phrases, you will be able to write sentences using prepositional phrases with 90 percent accuracy.

Now, in examining the chart in Figure 10-1, note that the lateral data explains the various classifications of knowledge, while the vertical data explains the various Thought Processes and their varied dimensions. To determine the value attributable to the student's classification of

BEHAVIORS		Terminology	Specific Facts	Conventions	Trends, Sequences	Classification, Categories	Criteria	Methodology	Principles & Generalizations	Theories & Structures
Evaluation in Terms of External Criteria	7.5									
Evaluation in Terms of Internal Evidence	7.0									
Derivation of a Set of Abstract Relations	6.7									
Production of a Plan or Operations Scheme	6.3									
Production of a Unique Communication	6.0									
Analysis of Organizational Principles	5.7									
Analysis of Relationships	5.3									
Analysis of Elements	5.0									
Application	4.0									
Extrapolation	3.5									
Interpretation	3.0									
Translation	2.0									
Remembering	1.0	2	3	4	5	6	7	8	9

K N O W L E D G E S

FIGURE 10-1.

EVALUATING BEHAVIORAL OBJECTIVES

knowledge we read the bottom of the chart from left to right until we reach an indication of what knowledge is expected of the student. Since he is being asked to become familiar with ways of treating sentence structure, this knowledge classification would most nearly meet the classification of "Conventions" which would receive a value of 3.0. Our next step is to determine which Thought Process is appropriate. Since the student is being asked to write sentences using prepositional phrases, this would involve the Thought Process of "Application." Reading the vertical indications of the chart from the base upwards, we are able to determine that the value of the Thought Process of Application is 4.0, and, by multiplying the two values, we have an end product of 12.0. If we were to consider this end product value in relation to the highest product which it is possible for the student to achieve, i.e., 67.5, upon dividing the latter figure by his end product value, we would come up with a Behavioral Objective for him evaluated at the 17th percentile. With this information available, it may be indicated that the Behavioral Objective for the student should be changed to one of a more formidable value.

Evaluating Attitudinal Response

It was mentioned previously that it is extremely difficult to evaluate the Affective Domain. However, at this point, the author would suggest one method for evaluating attitudes of students, as they relate to the Cognitive Domain, which has met with some success. Figure 10-2 consists of a chart by which the attitudinal response of a student is evaluated according to a 0 to 7 scale of +10 to +110. The following situation is described to demonstrate the use of the chart to evaluate a student's attitudinal response to a Behavioral Objective:

The Individual Study Unit which the student has completed included the following Behavioral Objective:

Behavioral Objective:

Given materials to read and study on split infinitives, you will be able to identify and correct these sentences with 90 percent accuracy.

The student has completed the Learning Experience, Self Evaluation Section and the required number of Learning Activity Options. He has responded to 92 percent of the questions in the Post-Test. In the section of his Individual Study Unit entitled "Attitudinal Objective" he was given the following examination question to examine his attitude on the subject:

Attitudinal Objective:

Examination Question—Now that you have completed this unit on Split Infinitives, what are your true feelings about the subject?

THOUGHT PROCESS

	Positive Response					Negative Response				
THOUGHT PROCESS	Characterization	Organization	Valuing	Responding	Receiving	Receiving	Responding	Valuing	Organization	Characterization
Evaluation	-110	100	-90	-80	-70	+70	+80	+90	+100	+110
Synthesizing	-100	-90	-80	-70	-60	+60	+70	+80	+90	+110
Analyzing	-90	-80	-70	-60	-50	+50	+60	+70	+80	+90
Application	-80	-70	-60	-50	-40	+40	+50	+60	+70	+80
Interpretation	-70	-60	-50	-40	-30	+30	+40	+50	+60	+70
Translation	-60	-50	-40	-30	-20	+20	+30	+40	+50	+60
Remembering	-50	-40	-30	-20	-10	+10	+20	+30	+40	+50

LEVELS OF ATTITUDE ATTAINMENT
FIGURE 10-2.
EVALUATING THE ATTITUDINAL DOMAIN

The student's answer to this question was:

Although I made a good mark on this subject, I didn't feel it was necessary for me to learn this unit. I don't split my infinitives and if I did, I think it sometimes puts more emphasis on what is being said. I really believe that it depends on the writer. Some good writers split their infinitives frequently. If it gets the message across, that's what counts—Doesn't it?

A sincere student,

The teacher examining this section on the Attitudinal Objective probably will be in a quandary as to how to evaluate the student's attitude. The important thing here is that he did very well on his Post-Test and this certainly should be foremost in the teacher's mind. In order to evaluate the student, if we refer to the chart in Figure 10-2, we must first determine which Thought Process was expected of him. We can determine this by examining the Behavioral Objective: We see that he was asked to recognize and correct those sentences which included Split Infinitives. In order to do this, he must be able to analyze the sentence and correct those sentences incorrectly constructed. Therefore, the Thought Process we are concerned with is "Analysis" which indicates a score from ±50 to ±90. Our next step is to decide what level of attitude the student actually attained. Referring back to his response to the Attitudinal Objective, we quickly see that he has placed value in the decision of the writer to split infinitives. He has his own conviction about the use of split infinitives and even though he may not have answered this question in the way the teacher desired, he must be respected for his opinion. In this case, the student's attitudinal response is a ±70 which places him in the 83rd percentile. Mathematically, his score was computed thusly:

First, the student was placed on a given level according to the Thought Process which was to be realized by the Behavioral Objective, which was in the ±50 to ±90 scale. Second, the teacher evaluated his response to the Attitudinal Objective and it was decided that the level of attainment reached by him was plus value. Third, it was then possible to place his attitudinal response at a plus 70. The total number of possible scores that he could make is 70, i.e., there are 70 boxes in the chart. The student placed 12 boxes below the highest score which means that he scored at 58. We now divide 70 into 58 and we arrive at a score in the 83rd percentile for him.

A point of concern here is that one limitation of this test is its subjectivity and the scoring is heavily dependent upon the teacher's evaluation of the student. However, almost any evaluation tool devised to examine attitude must, of necessity, be subjective to some extent. The teacher must bear in mind that perhaps her greatest contribution to a student will be to provide him with added knowledge and experience with which he can re-orient, change or re-direct his own inherent attitudes about a given subject.

SUMMARY

Evaluation is an essential part of any ongoing program. The contemporary teacher who assumes his new role in an individualized instructional program must be able to fulfill the role of a resource person, guidance counselor, a psychologist, a catalytic agent and a generalist. There are several basic principles which must be considered when evaluating a student:

1. The evaluation tool must determine the extent of the student's growth in terms of Cognitive Domain, Affective Domain and Psycho-Motor Skills;
2. The evaluation tool must indicate the progress of the student in terms of the Behavioral Objective;
3. Evaluation must be a continual process;
4. Varied evaluation strategies should be utilized;
5. Appropriate provision should be made for the recording of evaluative results in the Individual Study Unit;
6. Students should be encouraged to evaluate themselves. Evaluation in the Cognitive Domain involves the process of measuring the growth of students in terms of the Though Processes which relate to the specific Behavioral Objectives stated. Evaluation in the Affective Domain is usually subjective and extremely difficult to achieve effectively. However, both the Cognitive and Affective Domains can be evaluated in terms of their relative value to the total Thought Processes involved and the level of attitude attainment reached.

11

Containing Administration of the Individualized Instruction Program

Since previous chapters have dealt with the development of an instrument for the individualization of instruction so that the unique needs of each student can be met, it seems in order for this chapter to discuss the administration aspects of conducting an individualized instructional program, i.e.:

The Organization of the Classroom

Procedures for the Administration of
the Individualized Instruction Program

The Grouping Procedure for Individualizing
the Instructional Program

ORGANIZATION OF THE CLASSROOM FOR AN INDIVIDUALIZED INSTRUCTIONAL PROGRAM

There are two basic methods by which a school may be organized effectively to promote the individualization of instruction. The first and most common method is utilization of self-contained classrooms. The alternate method utilizes a cluster classroom arrangement. Each has its advantages and disadvantages, and both are discussed in some detail below.

Organization of the Self-Contained Classroom

The self-contained classroom is quite familiar to educators throughout the world. This classroom is organized in a manner which permits the strategic dispersal of various types of learning structures throughout a single room to accommodate the various needs of students engaged in differing Learning Activity Options. Figure 11-1 illustrates a typical self-contained classroom arrangement which has been organized for the individualization of instruction. Areas A and E are tables to accommodate a number of students working together on a similar project which may or may not be similar Learning Activity Options. Because there may be some verbal noise emanating from these areas, both tables have been separated and placed in opposite corners.

Areas B, D and G are designed to accommodate students working on the same options where there is a team learning experience. The options these students might be involved in could include making a tape together, writing a report, or any of the many options which require a student to work in a "buddy" arrangement.

Area C is for independent study. "Wet" and "Dry" study carrels are arranged within this area to allow independent study. A reference to the illustration will make it readily apparent to the reader that there are no arrangements in which students are grouped in the "traditional" arrangement of seats lined up in staid rows. Students who have opted to work independently are given that opportunity with a minimum of effort.

Area F provides a small group of students with the opportunity to discuss common options for which the requirement might be that they work together to create and produce something original, i.e., a skit, report, script, etc.

Area H is arranged to accommodate a group seminar or similar option. Caution must be exercised here so that the seminar discussion does not interfere with the rest of the classroom.

Additional furniture which might be located throughout the classroom would include a couch and a lounge chair resting on a carpet, where students might quietly read or browse through educational materials.

Medium group and large group instruction can be accomplished in this organizational pattern by utilizing the cafeteria, auditorium and, in certain situations, large open spaces in the school plant such as corridors or the basement.

Learning Centers, if not already established in the school plant, should be designed and created to afford students the opportunity of correcting deficiencies in a particular subject area. A Learning Center might be established each for Mathematics, English, Reading, or any other subject area. Educators planning to create Learning Centers in their own schools might first wish to visit other schools where Learning Centers have already been installed to observe their use and effectiveness.

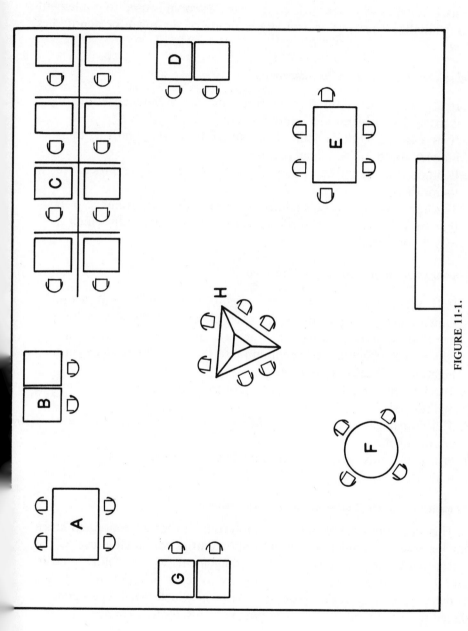

FIGURE 11-1.

ORGANIZATION OF SELF—CONTAINED CLASSROOM FOR THE INDIVIDUALIZATION OF INSTRUCTION

The reader must by now be aware that there exist several advantages and disadvantages where the self-contained classroom is used to implement an individualized instructional program. Some of these can be denoted as follows:

Advantages of the Self-Contained Classroom:

1. It can be a successful first venture into the individualization of instruction if organized as stated herein;
2. It is easy to control and direct students as they pursue their individualized instructional program;
3. It limits student traffic as they move from one grouping procedure to another.
4. Teachers may be more inclined to prefer this arrangement over that of the cluster classroom, because of the ease with which it may be operated.

Disadvantages of the Self-Contained Classroom:

1. It is expensive to initiate, if the organization is truly going to be individualized. For example, in each classroom, there may be a need to have two, three or four tape recorders, or any other educational machine, to accommodate the needs of students in a highly individualized program;
2. Teachers may tend to teach small groups if strict supervision is not maintained;
3. This organization is not as flexible as the cluster classroom arrangement;
4. Primarily, this arrangement can best be used in elementary schools.

Organization of the Cluster Classroom Arrangement

This classroom arrangement is preferred to the self-contained classroom because it provides maximum opportunities for flexible use of the physical plant. The cluster classroom arrangement, which is illustrated in Figure 11-2, is organized by arranging six to ten classrooms in a cluster and delineating a specific grouping pattern which each classroom is designed to accommodate. The grouping patterns allowed for are:

1. Independent Study
2. Small Group Instruction
3. Seminars
4. Medium Group Instruction

Similarly to self-contained classroom organization, the cafeteria and

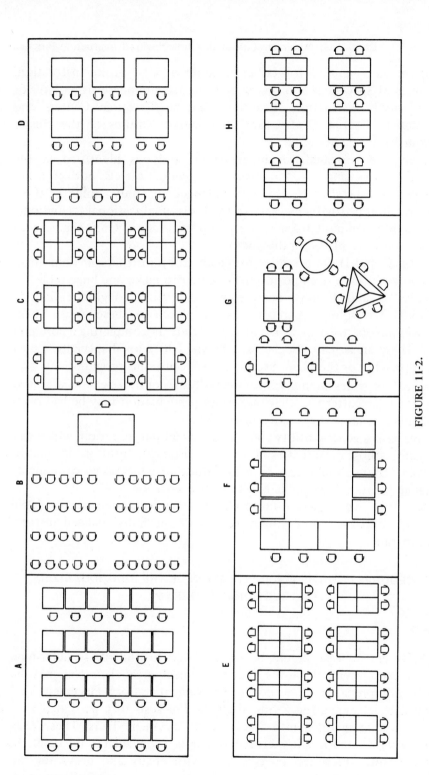

FIGURE 11-2.

ORGANIZATION OF CLUSTER CLASSROOMS FOR THE INDIVIDUALIZATION OF INSTRUCTION

auditorium can be used for either medium or large group instruction. Large areas of space can also be set aside to accommodate either large or medium group instruction. Learning Centers, Resource Centers and Instructional Material Centers are all essential features of the cluster classroom arrangement.

Area A is provided for independent study as identified in the Learning Activity Options. A number of individual carrels, both wet and dry, have been installed to facilitate independent study. Some of these carrels are equipped with a variety of the tools of educational technology.

Area B accommodates medium group instruction. Only chairs, with desks or tables, are placed in this room.

Areas C and H are arranged for small group instruction. Four small tables and desks have been positioned together to make one huge table.

Areas D and E have been equipped with a conglomeration of educational technology. Large tables are placed in these areas. These rooms can also be used as work areas for students completing a common option. These areas may also be used by the educational specialists, such as the art teacher or the science teacher, to execute this program.

Area F provides an area for seminars. Tables or desks can be arranged in a rectangular pattern so that maximum participation may be had from all students attending the seminar classroom.

Area G is a general utility room or a general purpose room which can be used for a host of activities. There is a variety of furniture located in this room. There should also be a multitude of educational equipment, supplies and materials available for student-teacher use.

Now that two suggested classroom patterns have been discussed, we may proceed to the actual administration of the individualized instructional program.

PROCEDURES FOR THE ADMINISTRATION OF THE INDIVIDUALIZED INSTRUCTIONAL PROGRAM

First Step

A Placement Test should be administered to students to determine their correct placement in the specific subject area. This test may be commercially prepared, an academic achievement test or a Placement Test developed by changing the forms of all the Pre-Tests of a particular Unit prior to combining them into several unit Placement Tests. These tests may be administered in a homeroom, or a large room such as the cafeteria or gymnasium, which can be equipped with chairs and desks for the purpose. Once the Placement Level of each student has been indicated, the results must be recorded on the student's Placement and Progress Report. This report is illustrated in Figure 11-3.

Second Step

Once the Student's Placement and Progress Report has been completed for all students, the teacher and her aide will distribute an Individual Study Unit folder and the appropriate Individual Study Unit to each student. The Individual Study Unit Folder is used to store the student's Individual Study Units. Each student is supplied with a bin in which he keeps his folder and all Individual Study Units.

Third Step

Now that students are supplied with their respective Individual Study Units, they initiate their Learning Experience by reading the Rationale and Behavioral Objective prior to determining whether or not they can successfully complete the Pre-Test. If a student cannot complete the Pre-Test, then the student reads the Learning Experience and selects those Learning Activity Options by which he desires to complete his Learning Experience. Once the student decides on those Learning Activity Options he will utilize, the teacher or teacher aide will check the desirable grouping procedure for the various options in the Master Grouping Procedure Booklet and denote the selections on the student's Learning Activity Options Selection Form. The Selection Form illustrated in Figure 11-4 is appropriate for use. Once this card is completed and signed by the teacher, the student should proceed to the appropriate study area within the self-contained classroom, or the appropriate room in the cluster classroom arrangement, depending on which grouping pattern is used.

Fourth Step

When the student has completed the Individual Study Unit, it has been evaluated by the student, and he has been successful in returning the specified minimum of correct responses, he requests from the teacher a Student's IS Unit Evaluation Form which the student will use to evaluate the Unit which he has just completed to determine its weaknesses and its strengths. The aforementioned form is illustrated in Figure 11-5.

Fifth Step

Although it is not necessary for the teacher to evaluate the effectiveness of each Individual Study Unit, it should be done when a teacher notices certain details about the Unit. The Unit might be too difficult; a

INDIVIDUAL STUDY UNIT
PLACEMENT AND PROGRESS REPORT

Student_____Teacher_____

Date_____ Subject_____

Skill		1	2	3	4	5	6	7	8	9	10	11	12	13
Level	A													
	B													
	C													
	D													
	E													
	F													
	G													
	H													
	I													
	J													
	K													

FIGURE 11-3.

STUDENT'S PLACEMENT AND PROGRESS REPORT

LEARNING ACTIVITY OPTIONS SELECTION FORM

STUDENT _____   DATE _____
HOME ROOM TEACHER _____   TIME _____
TITLE OF UNIT _____ SKILL/CONCEPT _____   LEVEL _____

Learning Activity Options	Grp. Proc.	Cls. Room	Sci. Lab.	Sp. Lab.	Aud.	Caf.	Gym.	Off.	Play Gr.	Sty. Ctr.	Comp. Lab.	Math Lab.
1.												
2.												
3.												
4.												
5.												
6.												
7.												
8.												
9.												
10.												
11.												
12.												

CODE: Independent Study—IS   Small Group Instruction—SG   Medium Group Instr.—MG
       Seminar—SE   Large Group Instruction—LG   Research—RE
       Tutoring—TU   Team Learning—TL   Out-of-School Proj.—OS

Checked by Teacher _____

FIGURE 11-4.

LEARNING ACTIVITY OPTIONS SELECTION FORM

STUDENT'S I.S. UNIT EVALUATION FORM

Student_____Date Completed_____

Now that you have successfully completed your I.S. Unit, we would like to know your opinion about this Unit. Your opinion will help us to improve this Unit if it is needed.

Title of I.S. Unit_____ Level_____

Skill Concept_____

1. Did you like this I.S. Unit?   Yes_____   No _____

                                                        No opinion _____

2. If your answer to no. 1 is "No," what is it that you did not like?

3. What did you like best about this Unit?

4. Do you think the I.S. Unit was too difficult?_____

5. Do you like this Unit better than a textbook?

6. What is your overall rating of this Unit? (Check one answer)

Super_____Excellent _____Good _____Fair _____Poor _____

When you have completed this form, return it to your teacher.

FIGURE 11-5.
STUDENT'S INDIVIDUAL UNIT EVALUATION FORM

particular option may rarely be chosen by a student; a Multiple Level Behavioral Objective may be too difficult; or a host of other flaws might exist which would point up imperfections in a Unit. So that effort to eliminate flaws and maximize the effectiveness of Individual Study Units is continuous, the teacher should be asked to evaluate the effectiveness of an Individual Study Unit when she feels that it is indicated by completing a Teacher's IS Unit Evaluation Form similar to the one appearing in Figure 11-6.

GROUPING PROCEDURES FOR INDIVIDUALIZING THE INSTRUCTIONAL PROGRAM

Grouping by interest is perhaps the most effective method of grouping students for the individualization of instruction. Gibson and Wilkens state:

> Interest as a criterion for grouping takes into account an important dimension of learning that grouping by ability and achievement may neglect, namely motivation. [1]

This is what takes place when students select their options; they also, in fact, select the grouping procedure which is determined by the particular act required or dictated by the option. Effective grouping procedures are built into the individualized instructional program when Individual Study Units are utilized in a school district. There are a number of grouping arrangements:

1. Independent Study

This grouping arrangement allows students to work independently without any interaction with other students. Usually, it is best that individual study carrels be set up to accommodate this grouping arrangement.

2. Small Group Instruction

This grouping arrangement is established when a number of youngsters are interacting on a common unit of study. The author will not insist on a particular number of students, but caution should be taken that the group does not become so large that its effectiveness is hampered by its size.

3. Seminar

---

[1] Gibson, Dorothy Westby and Wilkens, Fred T., *Grouping Students for Improved Instruction* (Englewood Cliffs, N.J.: Prentice-Hall, Inc., 1966), p. 29.

TEACHER'S I.S. UNIT EVALUATION FORM

Teacher _____Date_____

I.S. Unit Title_____Level_____

Skill or Concept_____

What are the weaknesses of this I.S. Unit?

What are the strengths of this I.S. Unit?

What recommendations do you offer for improving the effectiveness of this I.S. Unit?

What is your overall rating of this I.S. Unit? (check one)

Superior_____Excellent _____Good _____Fair _____Poor _____

FIGURE 11-6.

TEACHER'S I.S. UNIT EVALUATION FORM

This grouping arrangement is used when a number of students have arranged to meet and discuss a particular topic.

4. Medium Group Instruction

This grouping arrangement usually consists of forty to fifty students organized for the purpose of a lecture or a film, or some activity which is pertinent to a group of this size.

5. Large Group Instruction

This grouping arrangement usually accommodates a large number of students for lectures, films, demonstrations, etc.

SUMMARY

There are basically two arrangements for organizing the classroom for individualization of instruction:

1. The Self-Contained Classroom in which the instruction is limited to one classroom;
2. The Cluster Classroom composed of several classrooms, each one established to accommodate specific grouping arrangements.

There are five procedures for administering the individualized instructional program:

The first step is to administer the Placement Test to determine the student's Placement Level.

The second step consists of issuing Individual Study Units and Folders to each student.

In the third step, the student completes the Student's Learning Activity Options Selection Form and proceeds to the various stages to complete the Learning Experience.

For the fourth step, the student evaluates the effectiveness of the Individual Study Unit and submits the appropriate form to the instructor.

Finally, the teacher also approves the Individual Study Unit for its effectiveness.

There are several grouping techniques which may be employed to aid in the individualization of instruction.

APPENDIX A1

Sample Educational Instrument

Individual Study Units (ISU)

in use at

The Wyandanch Public Schools

Wyandanch, L.I., New York   11798

Language Arts / Social Studies

LOOK ALIKE WORDS

TEAR

TEAR

Study Skills

C   VOCABULARY DEVELOPMENT

   Homographs

WHAT AND WHY -

    This could be a very funny world if you didn't know the different meanings of look-alike words. You could, for example, have a tooth fall out of your gum.

You could have an ear of corn.

You could water your plant.

You could have a tear in your shirt.

    When you see look alike words, you must be able to picture the correct meaning of the word. In this unit, you are going to see how you can know the correct meaning of look alike words.

WHAT YOU WILL BE ABLE TO DO -

    At the end of this unit, which deals with the differences in meaning between look alike words, you should be able, with 80% accuracy, 1) to pick out words that look alike but have different meanings; 2) to draw pictures that show the meanings of look alike words.

PRE-TEST/SELF-TEST -

1. Words that look alike may have different meanings.
    Can you draw 2 pictures to show the different
    meanings of the word "wind?"

    1.   2.

    _____   _____

2. Can you write the 2 look alike words that these
    pictures stand for?

    1.   2.

    _____   _____

    1.   2.

    _____   _____

3. Many times, words with different meanings are spelled
    the same. These words_____alike.

4. Think of a look alike word and show two different
    meanings by drawing pictures.

5. There are many look alike words. See if you can
   think of five.

   1. _____

   2. _____

   3. _____

   4. _____

   5. _____

LEARNING EXPERIENCE -

When you read, you often see words
that look alike but mean different
things. A plant with leaves on it is
not the same as a plant that your
father may work in; but the words
look alike. When you read that the
plant had leaves, you pictured in
your mind....

When you read about a plant that people work in,
you may have pictured the C & D Cement Block Plant on
Booker Avenue.

Making a picture in your mind, helps you to know
the meaning of the word. All look alike words have
different meanings. Pictures help you to see the
different meanings of words.

<u>LEARNING ACTIVITY OPTIONS</u> -

Choose 3 out of 10 options. Put
a check (✔) next to the ones you
choose.

_____1. Make up other "funny world" pictures using look

alike words. To start you, how about a one foot

ruler.

_____2. For all your own funny world pictures and the

funny world pictures at the beginning of this

unit, show what they should look like in the

real world.

_____3. Listen to the tape on look alike words and
         read the paragraph that goes with the tape
         while you are listening. See if you recognize
         all the look alike words that are used. Write
         them here.

_____4. Watch the film on the look alike twins. See if
         you can appreciate how words that look alike
         "feel" when people don't recognize them.

_____5.   Pick out the look alike words from the drawings.
          Both drawings are different meanings for the
          look alike word.

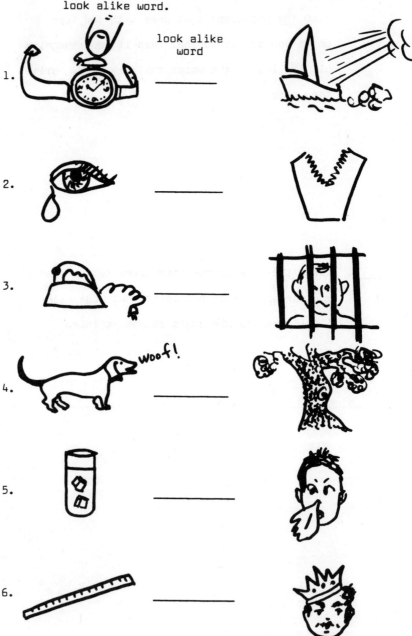

                                look alike
                                  word

1.   _____

2.   _____

3.   _____

4.   _____

5.   _____

6.   _____

7.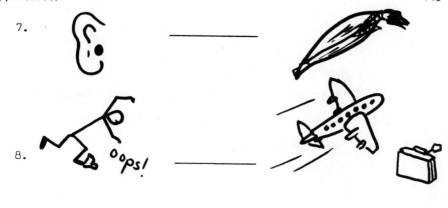

8.

9.

10.

_____ 6. Draw pictures to show the different meanings
        for these look alike words.

plant

ruler

trip

train

gum

_____7. Make up a list of look alike words. See how

many you can find. Ask your friends if they

can add to your list.

_____8. Play old maid with the look alike word cards.

Ask your teacher for the cards.

_____9. Look up some of the look alike words you find

in this unit and read their meanings in the

dictionary. Write them down here.

_____10. Write a story using look alike words - it can

be very short. After you have written it,

change the look alike words into pictures

to make the story easier to understand.

POST TEST -

1. There are many words that look alike but have

    different meanings._____
                              true or false

2. Draw 2 pictures to show the 2 different meanings

    of the look alike word "wind,"

    1.   2.

3. Write the look alike words that these pictures

    stand for.

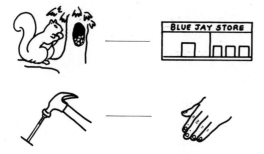

4. Words with different meanings that are spelled the

    same are look_____words.

5. Think of look alike words (2) and show their

    meaning by drawing pictures.

6.   Name 5 look alike words.

    1. _____

    2. _____

     3. _____

    4. _____

    5. _____

HOW DO YOU FEEL -

>   These questions ask you how you
>   feel about this unit.

1. Did you find that pictures help you to see the
    meaning of look alike words? Explain.

2. If instead of look alike words, we could have
    pictures would it be easier to understand what
    you are reading? Why?

3. If I ask you what the word "plant" means, would
    you be able to tell me only one thing. Why or
    why not?

<u>EVALUATION</u>

1. Does the student recognize that words that look
    alike can have different meanings.

2. Is the student able to visualize the difference
    in meaning between look alike words?

3. Is the student able to recognize look alike words
    outside the unit?

STUDENT_____

DATE_____

This student has successfully
completed this unit of work.

Teacher;_____

Date:_____19_____

Sample
Tri-Part Individual Study Units

IS Unit Script for Recording

IS Unit Picture Booklet

IS Unit Worksheet

in use at

The Wyandanch Public Schools

Wyandanch, L.I., New York 11798

LANGUAGE ARTS/SOCIAL STUDIES

IS UNIT SCRIPT FOR RECORDING

STUDY SKILLS

A—Vocabulary Development
Color Words—Red

WHAT AND WHY:

For this part of your IS Unit, you should have with you your worksheet, your picture book and a box of crayons. Look at the cover of your ISU picture book. (pause) The picture on the cover shows Johnny and his mother going into the Blue Jay Supermarket. The pictures in your work booklet tell about the story that I am going to read to you. When I tell you to, turn the page of your work booklet. Listen now to the story called "A Walk to Blue Jay's."

One day Johnny and his mother took a walk to the grocery store. Johnny's mother wanted to buy some fruit and she asked Johnny to help her choose it. Everyone in the family liked apples, so his mother asked him to pick out some nice red apples and put them in a bag. Turn the page. (pause) Johnny came back with a bag of fruit; but when his mother looked inside, she did not see red apples, she saw *green* apples. Turn the page. (pause) She told Johnny that these were not red apples but green apples. "The apples I want are red" she told him and showed him the color red on his shirt. Turn the page. (pause) He went over to the shelf and came back with a bag of big *red* apples.

When you have finished working with this unit, I want you to be able to pick out things that are red just like Johnny did, and to be able to pick out things that are not red whenever your teacher asks you to.

But before you begin learning about the color red, you will take a pre-test. If you do everything correctly, you will not have to continue with this unit. Open your worksheet to Page 1. Look for the numeral 1 on the bottom of the page. I'll wait. (pause) Open your box of crayons and with your red crayon draw a picture of an apple. Stop the player while you do that and then turn the player on again. Ready? Stop the player. (pause) Look at the pictures in your picture book and with your red crayon draw a circle around each picture that has the color red in it. After you have finished doing that, go to your teacher and tell her about something in your classroom that is red. Your teacher will check your pre-test. If you continue this unit begin listening to this tape at the frame number that begins part 2. (pause)

Open the box that the teacher in the Learning Center gave you. Put the lid on the bottom of the box.

Look in the box. You see a red crayon, a red block a piece of chalk and a pair of scissors. The chalk and the scissors are not red. The crayon and the block are red. Take out the two (2) red things and put them on the desk. Now open your workbook to page 2 and with your red crayon draw a picture of the block and color it in. Stop the player while you do this and then turn it back on. Ready? Stop the player. (pause)

Listen now while I tell you about some activities you can do to help you learn about the color red. I'm going to tell you about 3 activities and you will choose one of them to do now.

This is activity number 1.

On a piece of drawing paper, draw a picture of something red.

This is activity number 2.

Find a picture of something red in a magazine. Cut it out and give it to your teacher for the color bulletin board.

This is activity number 3. Play a game with a friend who is working on this unit. Show him or her 3 blocks. One must be red. The others should be different colors. Have your friend pick out the red block. Then your friend should let you have a turn to pick out the red block.

Remember, you must do one of these activities now. You may do activity 1 and draw something red, or activity 2 and cut a red picture out of a magazine or activity 3 and play the block game with a friend.

When you come back to continue this unit, start listening to this tape at the frame number that begins part 3. Ready? Stop the player. (pause)

Listen now while I tell you about some more activities that you can do to help you learn about the color red. You must choose one of them to do now.

This is activity number 4. Tell your teacher the name of one of your classmates who is wearing something red.

For activity number 5, draw a picture of something red that Johnny saw at Blue Jay's.

To do activity number 6, you must find something in your classroom that is red that you can put on your desk. Show your teacher.

Do one of these activities now and when you continue this unit, start listening to this tape at the frame number that begins part 4. Ready? Stop the player. (pause)

You are ready to do your next activity. Choose one of the following to do now.

This is activity number 7. Ask the teacher in the Learning Center to let you listen to the story of the "Little Red Hen." Then, use your red crayon and draw a picture of the little red hen.

Listen to activity number 8. Play the bean bag color game with two friends.

This is activity number 9. On one side of a piece of paper, paste two pictures of something red. Then turn the paper over and on the other side paste two pictures that do *not* have red in them.

After you have finished your activity, start listening to this tape at the frame number that begins part 5. (pause)

You are ready to take your post test. Turn to page 3 in your workbook. Draw a number that begins part 5. (pause)

You are ready to take your post test. Turn to page 3 in your workbook. Draw a picture with your red crayon Stop the player while you do this and then turn it back on. Ready? Stop the player. (pause)

On page 4 in your workbook, draw something that is *not* red. Stop the player while you do this and then turn it back on. Ready: Stop the player. (pause)

When you go back to your room, cut out a picture of something red from a magazine and paste it on page 4 of your workbook. Then put 6 red beads on a string from the beadbox and show them and your workbook to your teacher. Ready? Stop the player.

Now take your worksheet to your teacher and she will ask you some questions about how you liked the unit. Those questions are on page 5 of your worksheet. Show that page to your teacher and tell her you are ready for the questions.

IS UNIT WORKSHEET

(There are four blank sheets to this IS
Unit Worksheet on which the student will
record his assignments received via tape.)

WHAT DO YOU THINK?

1. Did you like learning about the color red? If you did, draw a picture of a big
   red apple. If you did not, make a sad red face.

2. Could you show another child in the room something that is red?

EVALUATION

1. Does the child know and understand the color red?

2. Comments:

Student name _____ Teacher _____

Date _____ Date _____

Sample

Individual Study Unit

"Macro" Unit

in use at

The Wyandanch Public Schools

Wyandanch, L.I., New York 11798

US

Language Arts / Social Studies

•Wyandanch

Study Skills
USING RESOURCE MATERIALS

MAPS — PHYSICAL

PURPOSE:

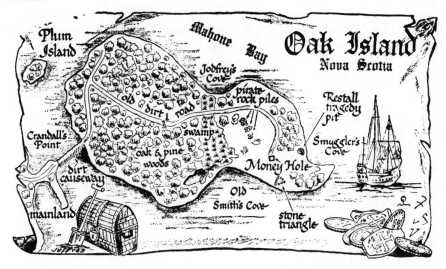

Pirates no longer sail the ocean blue, but many other people make maps today. You can never tell when you might have to produce a map. You have already studied several units on map techniques. Using the skills you have developed in those earlier units, you are going to be asked to develop one of two activities which will require you to use your knowledge in maps, so that you may have an opportunity to create something in map skills which has not existed before.

YOUR GOAL:

Given the information on how to construct a map, you will be able, with 90 percent accuracy, to:

1. Develop a map which has not existed before

or

2. Develop a manual on map symbols.

PRE-TEST

1. Write an essay describing how you would make a map on any location of your choice.

2. Describe the importance of direction, scale of miles and boundary lines in making a map.

3. Illustrate and explain twenty different map symbols.

4. Why do you think map symbols are important?

LESSON:

You have already studied several units on map skills. You might want to refer to these units during your study of map making.

It is easy to read a map—you should be able to do this without any difficulty. Making a map can be just as simple. Below is a map of the Babylon athletic field.

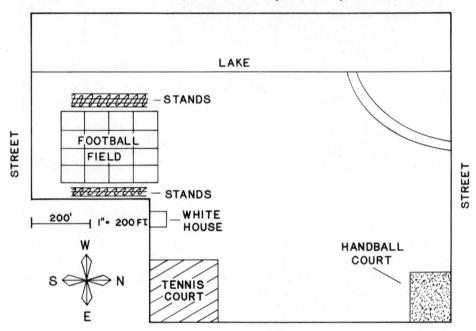

The map above is a "scale model drawing" of the athletic field at Babylon High School. I used several skills to draw this map. By using a tape measure I was able to measure the outside boundaries of the area I wished to place on the map. I also used the tape measure in order to calculate the length and width of the football field, the tennis court, the athletic house, and the handball court. What scale did I use? 1 inch equals 200 feet. You will need to decide on a scale when you make your map. I used boundary lines to show the borders of the map (streets and lake) and also to show the lines of the specific areas which I measured. Did you notice how easy it is to spot the specific areas I measured? This is because I made use of colors to show geographical locations (tennis court, handball court, etc.). Remember that this same skill is used in differentiating countries on a map. The drawn compass shows the directions on a map. I used a real compass to find out the directions on the athletic field. The needle on a compass always points to the north. You will need a compass when you draw your map. You now have learned how I used map skills to draw my map. Good luck when you draw yours.

Map symbols will enable you to determine at a glance specific objects which are man made or an act of nature. For example, objects which are in straight line form are usually man made. The following are some man made objects:

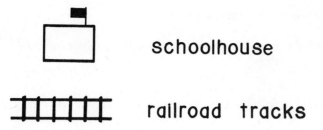

schoolhouse

railroad tracks

Objects which are not in straight line form are usually nature made, or not man made. Some of these objects are as follows:

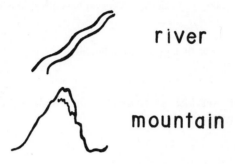

river

mountain

LEARNING ACTIVITY OPTIONS:

Choose any one of the following options to complete this Macro Unit. Check the one that you choose:

1. Get a compass and a tape measure from your teacher. You will also need a pencil and several sheets of paper.
   Make a map of Milton Olive School grounds. Include the school building, parking lot, basketball court, house and play area. You will need a tape measure in order to draw your map to scale. Use colored pencils to show the various areas on the school Grounds. Good luck.
2. Develop a manual entitled "Map Symbols." Your assignment is as follows:
   a. Decide on as many map symbols as you can think of and look them up in the school library.
   b. Decide on a code for each of these symbols.
   c. Alphabetize the symbols and code in a manual.
   d. Have your teachers check your work.
   e. Contact the art teacher and have him help you to design your cover.

POST-TEST FOR THE FIRST ACTIVITY:

1. What equipment do you need to draw a scale of an area?

2. Describe the steps you would follow in drawing a map of an area.

POST-TEST FOR THE SECOND ACTIVITY:

3. Produce your own symbols for ten of the symbols indicated in your manual on map symbols.

4. Indicate some symbols which may not be straight line form and may be man made.

YOUR OPINION:

1. Do you enjoy using the skills you have learned in other units? Why/Why not?

2. Do you feel that you were adequately prepared for this unit? Why/Why not?

3. Would you like to complete other units which are similar to this one? Why/Why not?

EVALUATION:

1. Can the student adequately develop a map?

2. Does the student understand the use of map symbols?

STUDENT_____   __Code:_____

DATE_____   This student has successfully completed
                                          this unit of work.

                                          _____
                                                         Teacher

                                          Date_____ 19 _____

Sample Educational Instrument

Individual Study Unit (ISU)

in use at

The Wyandanch Public Schools

Wyandanch, L.I., New York 11798

UNDERSTANDING MINORITY GROUPS

Individual Study Unit

Social Studies
Level D
(Unit 11)

RATIONALE:

We live in a pluralistic society.

Group problems can be solved through education and communication.

The culture in which a man lives influences his thoughts, values and actions.

Racism results from attributing hereditary superiorities to particular groups.

The purpose of this unit of study is to familiarize you with the problems confronting minorities and the majority group which demand better understanding so that some day all people will be able to live in harmony.

BEHAVIORAL OBJECTIVES:

Given opportunities to discuss minority groups in small groups, and upon the completion of this Individual Study Unit, you will be able, with 100 percent accuracy, to:

1. Identify difficulties and problems inherent among minority groups;
2. Identify difficulties and problems inherent among majority groups.
3. Recognize which inferences may be logically made regarding these difficulties and problems.

ATTITUDINAL OBJECTIVES:

1. To have an improved in-depth understanding of minority groups.
2. To recognize some of the problems which the majority group imposes upon minority groups.

PRE-TEST

Peruse this test to see if you can answer the questions successfully. If you can, complete all of the questions and submit the completed Pre-Test to your teacher for evaluation. If you find that you cannot answer all of the questions correctly, then proceed through the balance of this Individual Study Unit.

1. What is a ghetto?

2. What is meant by "equal opportunity"?

3. Why are some people prejudiced?

4. What do Jews and blacks have in common, if anything?

5. Does skin color make a difference in people?

6. Define the word "discrimination."

7. What is meant by the term "mainstream"?

LEARNING EXPERIENCE

For the past four hundred years, people have been coming to America from different lands. Each group had different reasons for coming here. The first generation of immigrants faced problems in being accepted into the mainstream of American life. Later generations seldom, if ever, felt different from other people in the country. Today, most of their problems have been solved.

There are, however, large groups of people who have been in America for many, many years and are still not accepted into the mainstream of American life. Afro-Americans, Mexican-Americans, American Indians, and Puerto Ricans are minority groups still having difficulties. These groups have not had equal opportunities to develop the best of their ideas and talents. They have been the victims of prejudice.

LEARNING ACTIVITY OPTIONS:

In order to continue your learning experience, you are to choose three of the seven Learning Activity Options which follow. Place a check mark next to the option which you have chosen and follow the instructions given.

Each of the following options is to be discussed in small groups. Next to each of the options, you will note a room number to which you will go to complete the option which you have chosen. When your group has formed, a chairman should be selected who will be responsible for directing the discussion group and making certain that each member of the group understands the question and is able to complete it. The chairman will be responsible for giving a presentation to the entire class when it has re-assembled in its original room 103.

(Room 104) 1. Develop a questionnaire to find out what people really know and think about skin color. Students may question friends and adults. A sample follows:

   A. Why do some people have different skin color?
   B. Is skin color important?
   C. Have you ever known of an incident when skin color affected a situation?
   D. Does skin color affect intelligence or personality? How do you know?
   E. Why do people like to get a suntan?

(Room 105) 1. Develop a vocabulary list related to discrimination, which should include the following:

color	prejudice
melanin	minority
pigment	equality
freedom	ghetto
discrimination	equal opportunity

(Room 106) 3. Develop an understanding of the confining nature and origin of the ghetto. Discuss the following excerpt with the group:

   The word "ghetto" comes from sixteenth-century Italy where Pope Paul IV decreed that "Jews shall live entirely separated from Christians, in a quarter or a street with one entrance and exit." The Jewish quarter, which the Venetians named a ghetto, had high walls separating it from the rest of the city. At night, its heavy gate was locked and only Jews with special passes were allowed outside. "America's black ghettos separated people because of their color rather than their religion. Negroes could not move 'up-town' even if they had the rent money." *(Tear Down the Walls–A History of the American Civil Rights Movement,* Dorothy Sterling, Doubleday, N.Y., 1968, pp. 113-115.)

A. Does the word "ghetto" pertain to Negroes only?
B. What do you think would be another appropriate term for the word "ghetto"?
C. Does the word "ghetto" offend you? Why?
D. Is there a white "ghetto"? If so, where?
E. Does the word "ghetto" imply that its residents are poor?

(Room 107) **4.** Discuss and be prepared to report on the following:

- Why some immigrants come to America.
- What problems they may have encountered.
- Why some groups were accepted and others not.
- Examples of "non-acceptance" known to students.
- Dictionary definition of prejudice.
- The meaning of the following terms:

Immigrants	Minority
Mainstream	Prejudice
Generation	Equal Opportunity

(Room 108) **5.** Develop an understanding of an example of prejudice as it affected a group of people. Read *The Picture Life of Martin Luther King, Jr.* Focus on the Montgomery, Alabama, boycott and Mrs. Rosa Parks.

(Room 109) **6.** Each person in the group shall have an opportunity to read sections from *Red Man, White Man, African Chief,* by Margaret Rush Lerner, to find out what melanin is and how it influences skin pigmentation.

(Room 110) **7.** The Speakerphone has been set up in this room. Arrangements have been made for your group to speak to Dr. Jerome Holland, former President of Hampton Institute, Hampton, Virginia, who has just been appointed to the post of Ambassador to Sweden. Your group will have forty-five minutes to discuss the questions you would like to pose to him about minority groups. Jot down these questions and each member of the group shall have an opportunity to ask one question. The teacher will come into the room a few moments before the interview is scheduled to set up the appropriate equipment.

POST-TEST:

Now that you have completed the Learning Activity Options, you are ready for the Post-Test. Answer all of the questions correctly.

1. Identify five problems confronting minority groups.

2. Why do you think these problems exist?

3. Do you believe that you now have an improved in-depth understanding of minority races? Why?

4. Has this made you into a better human being? How?

EVALUATION

The student is expected to score 90 percent correct answers. Questions numbered 1 and 2 are to be scored at ten points for each correct answer. The teacher should jot down any positive or negative comments verbally stated by the student during their conference together, concomitantly indicating his own commitments regarding the student's answer or comment.

APPENDIX B

Sample Educational Instrument

Contract

in use at

The Duluth Public Schools

Duluth, Minnesota 55802

UNIT: PREHISTORIC TIMES–EARLY MAN
NUMBER: 2

NAME _____
PERIOD _____
DATE: _____

PURPOSE: To establish a time place concept skill.

CITERION PERFORMANCE:

The student shall correctly place the following events on a time line.

a. Old Stone Age Began

b. New Stone Age Began

c. Village Life Began

d. The Bronze Age Began

e. Recorded History Began

f. River Valley Civilization Began

SAMPLE TEST ITEM:

Select the letter on the time bar which identifies the date of each of the events listed below. Write the correct letter in the blank before each event.

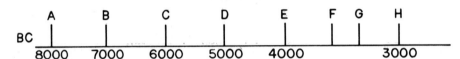

```
        A       B       C       D       E     F   G     H
BC      |       |       |       |       |     |   |     |
       8000    7000    6000    5000    4000          3000
```

_____Village Life Began

_____Old Stone Age Began

CRITERION PERFORMANCE:

Given a list of 10 developments of early man, the student will be able to classify them, in written form, according to the period in which they originated.

That is: a. Old Stone Age   b. New Stone Age   C. Bronze Age

SAMPLE TEST ITEM:

Write in the blank before each numbered statement the letter of the correct time period in which the statement occurred.

a. Old Stone Age   b. New Stone Age   c. Bronze Age

_____ The potter's wheel was invented.

_____Neanderthal man probably belongs to this period.

INSTRUCTIONAL PROCEDURE:

_____ Read and Do: in *Follett* lessons on p. 8-11.

_____ Read: in *Pageant* p. 2-8.

_____ Read: in *History of Our World* p. 26-45.

_____ View Film: *Prehistoric Times–Story of Man*

_____ View Filmstrips: *Old Stone Age, The Rise of Settled Village Life, New Stone Age, Birth Place of Civilization.*

_____ Do the teacher prepared worksheet.

WORKSHEET

I. Define the terms:
   a. prehistoric
   b. primitive
   c. self-sufficient
   d. civilization

II. Time line. Make a time line. . . . Show the following events on it.
   a. Old Stone Age Began   b. New Stone Age Began
   c. Village Life Began   d. The Bronze Age Began
   e. Recorded History Began   f. River Valley Civilization Began

III. Man's early history is broadly divided into three time periods according to the kinds of materials which he used for tools and weapons. The key below lists these three periods. Write in the blank before each numbered statement the letter of the correct time period.

   a. Old Stone Age   b. New Stone Age   c. Bronze Age

_____ 1. The potter's wheel was invented.
_____ 2. Hunting was the only method of making a living.
_____ 3. Men first began to plant and harvest crops.
_____ 4. Men began to carry on overseas trade.
_____ 5. Neanderthal man probably belongs to this period.
_____ 6. Animals were tamed and kept for food and labor.
_____ 7. This age began about 5,000 years ago.
_____ 8. The different languages of the world had their beginnings.
_____ 9. This was the longest of the three periods listed.
_____10. New ways of making a living led to the growth of villages.
_____11. Tools were made by chipping and flaking pieces of flint.
_____12. Men developed systems of writing.
_____13. Men learned to combine copper and tin to make a more useful metal.
_____14. Men learned to control fire and to use spoken language.
_____15. Men learned to water their fields by irrigation.
_____16. This age is believed to have begun about 10,000 years ago.

IV. Matching

		a.	Anthropologist
_____ 1.	People who travel from place to place.	b.	Archeologism
_____ 2.	Scientists who dig up and study remains from the past.	c.	Barrows
		d.	Erosion
_____ 3.	Name given to the period during which man left no written records.	e.	Geologists
		f.	Ice Age
_____ 4.	Scientists who study groups of human beings and how they live.	g.	Morainen
		h.	Nomads
_____ 5.	Rubbish heaps left by glaciers.	i.	Prehistoric
_____ 6.	Remains of primitive people are found in these burial mounds.	j.	Primitive
		k.	Self-sufficient
_____ 7.	This process gives us a clue to the age of the earth.	l.	Strata

_____ 8. Layers of rock and soil.
_____ 9. Scientists who study rock formations.
_____ 10. Describes someone who provides for all his own
            needs.

V. Write in the blank before each of the following statements the letter of the term or
phrase in parentheses which makes the statement true and complete.

_____ 1. The last great ice sheet (a. left glaciers in some parts of the world) (b. disap-
            peared completely).

_____ 2. We know that man (a. did) (b. did not) exist before the last great ice sheet.

_____ 3. Man has left written records for only the last (a. 50,000) (b. 5,000) years.

_____ 4. Nomads (a. lead a settled life) (b. wander over a large area).

_____ 5. The New Stone Age began about (a. 3,000) (b. 8,000) years before the first.

_____ 6. The New Stone Age was a (a. shorter) (b. longer) period than the Old
            Stone Age.

APPENDIX C

Sample Educational Instrument

Teaching Learning Unit (TLU)

in use across the nation

(Project Plan)

Developed and Produced by

The Westinghouse Learning Corporation

10-558   **MODULE TEST**   69-70 Ed.

Directions: Your teacher will grade this test for you. Before you begin, prepare a Performance Test Card for your teacher to use later. Write your *Student Number* and the *Module Number* for this test (10-558) and blacken the appropriate space below each number. Double-check to be sure that each box and space has been filled in correctly. All other marks on this card will be made by the teacher.

For Module 10-558 you were to choose a topic, gather related materials, study the proper procedures, and prepare and deliver a five-minute speech demonstrating voicing techniques.

Go back over the speech that you prepared, and restudy the criticisms that were made of it. Correct all errors and prepare to give it again. (Or if you prefer, you may prepare a new speech.)

When you are ready, ask your teacher when you may deliver it in the presence of your teacher and, if possible, some of your classmates.

END OF TEST

CHECK YOUR WORK. Be sure your Student Number and the Module Number for this test (10-558) have been correctly marked on your test card. When you have finished, take the Performance Test Card to the teacher.

10-558   **TEACHER DIRECTIONS**   69-70 Ed.

MODULE TEST 10-558

For this test, the student is to prepare a speech and deliver it in your presence and, if possible, that of some of his classmates. He may either use the speech that he prepared in the course of his work on the module, or, if he prefers, prepare a new one.

Listen to his speech and then answer the following questions. Mark answer space

        A if your answer to the question is YES; or

        B if your answer to the question is NO.

The number of the question corresponds to the row to be marked on the test card.

1. Does the student show normal poise or confidence?
2. Does he seem eager to share his ideas?
3. Does he seem to be sincere?
4. Does he have a good attitude toward himself?
5. Does he have a good attitude toward his audience?
6. Has he made a good choice of material to be included in his speech?
7. Has he found adequate material?

8. Is his material accurate?
9. Is his material interesting?
10. Is his material well organized?
11. Is his material well adapted to the audience and the occasion?
12. Is his speech suitable for the purpose?
13. Does his speech have an effective introduction?
14. Is his choice of words good?
15. Does his speech have an effective conclusion?
16. Does he maintain adequate eye contact?
17. Does he make normal use of facial expression?
18. Is his posture good?
19. Does he make suitable use of gestures?
20. Does he use movement from one place to another on the platform?
21. Is the pitch of his voice satisfactory?
22. Does he vary his pitch from time to time?
23. Is the quality of his voice satisfactory?
24. Is the loudness of his voice such that it reaches to the rear row of his audience?
25. Is his articulation good?
26. Is his pronunciation good? (Do not regard regional speech as mispronunciation.)
27. Is his rate of speech normal, except where speed is suitable to the subject matter?

When you have recorded your evaluation of the test card, submit it for computer scoring.

(0,00)
69-70 Ed.

MODULE NUMBER 10-558

OBJECTIVES
VOICING TECHNIQUES

6030 Given a choice of topic, related materials, and a list of procedures, select, prepare, and deliver a five-minute speech demonstrating voicing techniques.

10-558-2   (0,00)

INSTRUCTIONAL GUIDE

In order to do this unit, you will need to combine skills which you developed in previous units with a new skill: that of carefully controlling the sound of your voice. You have reviewed ways of gathering material for a speech and ways of designing your speech to suit your purpose, and you have also practiced several vocal exercises. The real test of whether or not you have successfully completed this unit will be your five-minute speech. Below, you will find a list of speech topics from which you may choose. These topics should be related to your reading; your speech should show that you have done some careful reading as well as mastered several techniques of

VOICING TECHNIQUES

10-558-2   (0,00)

ITEM	USE	DO	SELF-CHECK	DONE
1.	Module 10-556	1. Review Module 10-556.	How should I gather material for a speech? How should the purpose of a speech affect what is said and how it is said?	
2.	<u>Modern Speech</u>, by Irwin.	2. Read pages 60-69. Do all of the Activities included in these pages.	Have I improved the pitch, quality, and loudness of my voice?	
		3. Read pages 72-75 and do the Activities included in these pages	Have I improved my articulation?	
3.	<u>Modern Speech</u>, by Irwin.	4. Read pages 76-83 5. Read pages 90-93.	Have I improved my pronunciation?	
4.	<u>Instructional Guide</u>	6. Read the instructions. Prepare and deliver the required five minute speech. I.G.	Have I presented a successful speech?	

successful speaking. Choose a topic. Review the reading you have done in the literature program to gather material for your speech. Note the purpose of the topic you have chosen, and design your attack to suit this purpose. Give your speech for several of your classmates who are studying or have already studied this unit. Ask them to use the attached evaluation speech to evaluate your performance. Use their evaluation to decide whether or not you have successfully completed the unit.

Speech Topics

1. Retell a story from the viewpoint of one of the characters, showing how this character's viewpoint influences the story. If the story is already told by one of the characters choose a different character. (to inform)
2. Compare the main character of a biography with an outstanding person in your community who is in the same field. (to inform)
3. Tell why a character would or would not make a good friend. (to persuade)
4. Tell why you believe that after a certain point in a story there is only one way in which the story could possibly end. (to persuade)
5. Present a review of your favorite of the books you have read in the literature program this year. (to entertain)
6. Retell a humorous passage from a story in the literature program. (to entertain)

7. Convince your listeners that they should read a certain book. (to persuade)
8. Support the following statement: "Reading biographies is more worthwhile than reading most other types of books." (to persuade)
9. Describe an experience you have had which is similar to one described in one of the books you read this year. (to inform)
10. Explain how a character in a book illustrates what courage is. (to inform)

Evaluation Sheet

1.	choice and organization of material included in speech	1	2	3	4	5
2.	suitability of speech to purpose	1	2	3	4	5
3.	pitch of voice	1	2	3	4	5
4.	loudness of voice	1	2	3	4	5
5.	quality of voice	1	2	3	4	5
6.	articulation	1	2	3	4	5
7.	pronunciation	1	2	3	4	5

Circle the number of points you think the speaker should receive in each area. Five is the highest possible score; one is the lowest. A total score of 30-35 points is excellent. 25-30 is good. 20-25 is average, and 18-20 is below average. Anything less than 18 is unsatisfactory and indicates that the speaker needs more practice on this unit.

(0,00)

69-70 Ed.

MODULE NUMBER 10-558

OBJECTIVES

VOICING TECHNIQUES

6030 Given a choice of topic, related materials, and a list of procedures, select, prepare, and deliver a five-minute speech demonstrating voicing techniques.

10-558-3   (0,00)

INSTRUCTIONAL GUIDE

This unit requires that you combine skills acquired in previous TLU's with a new skill: mastery of vocal techniques. In order to do this, you have reviewed ways of gathering material and ways of adapting speech form to purpose and you have practiced various vocal techniques. The real test of whether or not you have successfully accomplished this unit will be your five-minute speech. Below, you will find a list of speech topics from which you may choose. These topics should be related to your reading in the literature program; your speech should show that you have done some thoughtful reading as well as mastered several rhetorical techniques. Choose a topic. Decide the purpose of that topic. Review your reading in order to gather material. Prepare and deliver a five-minute speech for several of your classmates who are studying or have already studied this unit. Ask them to use the attached evaluation sheet to evaluate your performance. Use their evaluation to decide whether or not you have successfully completed this unit.

VOICING TECHNIQUES

10-558-3   (0,00)

ITEM	USE	DO	SELF-CHECK	DONE
1.	Module 10-556	1. Review Module 10-556	How should I gather material for a speech? How should the purpose of a speech affect what is said and how it is said?	
2.	Speech in Action, by Robinson.	2. Read Chapter 9. Do all of the exercises at the end of the Chapter.	Have I improved in each of the following areas? breathing pitch and rate rate and time volume and force	
3.	Speech in Action, by Robinson.	3. Read Chapter 10. Do all of the exercises at the end of the chapter.	Have I improved my articulation and pronunciation?	
4.	Instructional Guide	4. Read the instructions in the I.G. Prepare and deliver the required five-minute speech.	Have I presented a successful speech?	

Speech Topics

1. Retell a story from the viewpoint of one of the characters, showing the influence of that character's personality on the seeming "truth" of the story. (If the story already is narrated by a character, choose another character.)
2. Compare the subject of a biography with an outstanding person in your community who is in the same field.
3. Tell why a character would or would not make a good friend.
4. Tell why you believe that after a certain point in a story there is only one possible outcome.
5. Retell a humorous passage in a story.
6. Present a review of your favorite of the books that you have read this year in an entertaining way.
7. Convince your listeners that they should read a certain book in the literature program.
8. Support the following statement: "Biographies are more valuable to read than most other kinds of books."
9. Tell about a personal experience which evoked feelings similar to those presented by an author.

10. Explain how a character in a book illustrates one or more of the traits that make up courage.

Evaluation Sheet

1.	choice and organization of material included in speech		1	2	3	4	5
2.	suitability of speech to purpose		1	2	3	4	5
3.	pitch of voice		1	2	3	4	5
4.	loudness of voice		1	2	3	4	5
5.	quality of voice		1	2	3	4	5
6.	articulation		1	2	3	4	5
7.	pronunciation	Total Score_____	1	2	3	4	5

Circle the number of points you think the speaker should receive in each area. Five is the highest possible score; one is the lowest. A total score of 30-35 points is excellent, 25-30 is good, 20-25 is average, and 18-20 is below average. Anything less than 18 is unsatisfactory and indicates that the speaker needs more practice on this unit.

(0,00)

69-70 Ed.

MODULE NUMBER 10-558

OBJECTIVES
VOICING TECHNIQUES

6030 Given a choice of topic, related materials, and a list of procedures, select, prepare, and deliver a five-minute speech demonstrating voicing techniques.

10-558-4   (0,00)

INSTRUCTIONAL GUIDE

Speech Critique Sheet

Speaker:

Topic:

Minimum and Maximum Time:

Area for evaluation	*Grade*	*Area for evaluation*	*Grade*
I. *Attitude and Preparation*		II. *Composition*	
(a) Poise		(a) Effective introduction	
(b) Confidence		(b) Choice of words	
(c) Preparation		(c) Organization of ideas	
(d) Eagerness to share ideas		(d) Adaptation of material	
(e) Sincerity		to audience and occasion	
(f) Enthusiasm		(e) Effective conclusion	
(g) Attitude toward self			
(h) Attitude toward class			

VOICING TECHNIQUES

10-558-4   (0,00)

ITEM	USE	DO	SELF-CHECK	DONE
1.	Modern Speech, By Irwin and Rosenberger.	1. Read pages 33-37, "Telephone Conversations."		
2.	Modern Speech, By Irwin and Rosenberger. Tape recorder.	2. Read pages 60-83: "You and Your Voice," "You and Your Articulation," "Improving Pronunciation."	Read words on page 74 into tape recorder. Replay, listen. Ask one of your classmates to help you when you come to this exercise.	
3.	Modern Speech, by Irwin and Rosenberger. Tape recorder.	3. Read pages 233-238, "How to Impress Others Audibly." Read pages 396-425, "Voice Quality."	Read a selection or two into tape recorder. Listen with your partner. Ask one of your classmates to help you when you come to this exercise.	
4.	Instructional Guide	4. Choose your topic and outline—check on S.C.S. if your teacher approves it.		
5.			Give the speech.	

III. *Delivery*

    (a) Eye contact
    (b) Facial expression
    (c) Posture
    (d) Gestures and movement
    (e) Focal projection
    (f) Speech rate

IV. *Content*

    (a) Information and ideas
    (b) Adequacy of material
    (c) Accuracy of material

Additional Comments:

Legend 1 = Unsatisfactory, 2 = Poor, 3 = Adequate, 4 = Good, 5 = Excellent

10-558-4   (0,00)

-2-

Topics for speech

1.   Select any piece of prose or poetry and read it aloud.

2. Assume you are nominating someone at the Republican or Democratic National Convention for the office of President of the United States of America.
3. Assume you are a T.V. announcer presenting a vital news flash.

Sample Educational Instrument

Unipac

in use across the nation

Sponsored by

Institute for Development of Educational Activities

UNIPAC Center

12345 Westminister

Santa Ana, California 92903

AN APPLE TREE HAPPENING

LEARNING OBJECTIVES

A. After observing visuals of an apple tree changing during the seasons of the year, the student will create something in art.
B. After observing a visual of an old apple tree, the student will create something in art.
C. After imagining or viewing an apple tree standing alone, the student will create something in art.

PRE-TEST

INSTRUCTIONS:

Go to your teacher who will give you an oral pre-test on this **UNIPAC**. Your teacher will tell you if you are to continue with this **UNIPAC**. If you did not complete the pre-test successfully, do not be discouraged. Find out why you were not successful.

PURPOSE OF THE PRE-TEST

The purpose of this pre-test is to find out how much you know about the changes an apple tree goes through during the four seasons of the year, how an old apple tree looks to you, and how an apple tree standing alone looks to you.

PRE-TEST

Here are the questions your teacher will ask you. Perhaps you would like to think about them before you see your teacher.

1. How do you think an apple tree looks in the fall?
2. How does an apple tree look in the winter?
3. How does an apple tree look in the spring?
4. How does an apple tree look in the summer?
5. How does an old apple tree look to you?
6. Tell me how an apple tree standing alone looks to you.

LESSON I

OBJECTIVE:

After observing visuals of an apple tree changing during the seasons of the year, the student will create something in art.

INSTRUCTIONS:

Choose any one of the activities listed under **HELPFUL IDEAS** which might help you get a better idea of the changes an apple tree goes through during the four seasons. When you feel you have an idea of the changes that an apple tree makes during the four seasons of the year, do any of the activities under **THINGS TO DO.**

See HELPFUL IDEAS and THINGS TO DO, below and on page 195.

HELPFUL IDEAS

LOOK AT:

Films	"A Plant Through the Seasons"
	"Washington State, Appleland"
	"A Tree Is a Living Thing"
	"Tomorrow's Trees"
	"The Physical Environment"
	"Children Who Draw"
	"Paper Sculpture" (5 min.)
	"Paper Sculpture" (22 min.)
	"Water Color"
	"Discovering Creative Pattern"
	"Discovering Line"
	"Discovering Texture"
	"What Will Clay Do"
	"Mural Making"
Photographs	6 photographs about apple trees,
	Washington State Apple Commission
Filmstrips	"Primary Art Series"
	"Rock Paintings"
	"Seeing Trees and Clouds"
Sound	"Composition in Nature"
Filmstrips	"Draw Big"
	"Learning to Look"
	"Listening, Looking, Feeling"
Slides	"Trees of Washington, Part I"
	"Trees of Washington, Part II"
	"Farming East of the Cascades I and II"
	20 slides on apples
Film Loops	"Pencil and Pen"
	"Paint "
	"Paper"
	"Collage"
	"Clay"
	"Construction"

READ:

Books	*Adventures in Stitches*
	Block and Silk Screen Printing
	Crafts Design
	Creative Clay Design

Creative Drawing
Creative Expressions with Crayons
Creative Paper Design
Creative Teaching in Art
Creating with Paper
Everyday Art "Little Girls and Big Stitches"
In the Elementary School
School Arts "Stitching a Mural"
The Arts in the Classroom
The Process of Art Education
The Stitches of Creative Embroidery
The Story of Washington Apples

GO: Field Trips
                 Parks
                 Neighborhood Community
                 Farm
                 Supermarket
                 Tree Farm

LISTEN TO: Music
                 "Shake The Apple Tree"
                     by Carl Reinecke—Ginn
                 Cherry Blossoms

DO: Poem—Write an Original Poem
                 Song—Write an Original Song
                 Dance—Make Up a Tree Dance
                 Riddle—Make Up Riddles About Trees
                 Cut Outs—From Magazines Make a Notebook on Trees.
                 Display—Gather Samples and Make a Nature Study Display.

GLOSSARY

Words have different meanings. These words used in this UNIPAC have a special meaning. If you need more help in knowing what a word means, look it up in the dictionary. Ask your teacher.

EFFECT—the way something looks, the way you want something to come out

INTERLOCK—like putting your fingers together and holding them together so they don't slip out

ATTACH—to put on, to paste on, to clip it on, to stick it on, to hold on to something else

UPRIGHT—placed up, not tipped, straight without falling

ENAMEL—a thick paint used after tempera or water color paint has dried to give it that shiny look, sometimes has a strong smell

TEXTURE—things like dots, checks you put on design to fill in empty places; things you can feel on the surface of objects

BALSA WOOD—soft, light wood that is used for models; it breaks very easily

CONSTRUCTIONS—to build, to put together, something you have made with your hands mostly

COLLECTION—objects of the same kind, different things gathered and saved to be used later or when you need them

SELF-EXPRESSION—the way you feel about something and how you show this feeling by doing something with it

OBSERVING—looking, studying something

ACTIVITIES—something you can try out on your own, something you might do to find out what happens

STRUCTURES—could be something that has shape and form, it could have sides

BALANCE—to hold still without one side falling

SUPPORTED—held up so it won't fall

THINGS TO DO

1. DRAWING

Any size, color paper may be used. Large crayons, chalk, felt pen and cut paper can be used in many different ways.

It might be easier to draw large forms first, then add texture or small things later. Try filling up the paper. Make things look closer and/or farther away.

Draw your own way. Try not to copy other people's ways of drawing. Draw the way you feel. Keep trying if you do not like it one way.

a. CRAYON RESIST

When drawing a picture or design, use light and bright colors on white or colored paper. Press down hard on the crayon. Then, over this drawing, paint with blue, purple or black water color. The dark color should bring out the bright colors underneath.

b. CRAYON ON CLOTH

Using a crayon, draw a picture or design on cloth. Press hard on the crayon. Next, place the cloth design side down on a newspaper and iron the back side of the design. The cloth can be of any size.

2. PAINTING

a. TEMPERA

Easy to use. Large paper and long brushes are easier to paint with. Mix paint thick so it will not drip. When mixing, add water to the powder paint, not powder to the water.

Put some newspapers under your painting to keep things neat.

b. WATER COLOR

White drawing or manila paper is easy to work on. Paper may be wet all over or in parts with a brush or sponge. Try different ways of painting.

Mix the colors on the paper while it is still wet. If you want to add texture, wait until the wet places are dry.

Dripping paint from the brush, tipping the paper, blowing the wet paint around can bring surprises you never planned.

Use light and quick strokes to keep colors clear and crisp. Brushing over one place too many times can give a muddy look.

Try rolling, turning or twisting the brush and see what happens on the paper.

For thick lines, use the side part of the brush. For thin lines, try the point and drag lightly across the page. Use the point of the brush to make dots for texture. Try to make the brush do the work for you.

3. SCULPTURE

a. PAPER MACHE

Paper mache is wet paper used with paste. The paste is flour and water, or wheat paste. There are three ways to make paper mache structures.

(1) Paper can be modeled like clay.

(2) Paper can be used over things: bottles, globes, balloons, newspaper coils and wire.

(3) Paper can be pressed into a mold to form a thin shell.

Once the basic shape is done, put better paper on top to give a smooth surface. Then paint and lacquer it, after it is dry.

b. WIRE

Shapes can be formed out of wire. Use a wire that can be bent, like: piano wire, clothes hangers, coils, binding wire or bailing wire. Be sure the wire form has a base to stand on. Bunch up the wire to make the form; or use the wire as you would a stick.

c. TWIGS OR STICKS

Twigs can be glued to make a form. Twigs or sticks can be pasted down on paper or cardboard to make a form. A form that stands alone should be a sound structure.

Twigs can be used for a tree with tissue or construction paper leaves and flowers glued to it. They can be held upright on a table by chunks of clay. The bare twigs can be painted with enamel colors.

d. PAPER

Paper can be made into a free standing form. Use a heavy paper that can be bent or cardboard.

You can slit two pieces into the center, then fit them together at right angles (see "Creating With Paper"). You can interlock pieces with slits.

Two flat shapes that are the same can be fastened in the middle with needle and thread, then spread apart.

You can start with a basic cone shape and then add fringe, curled paper, or crumbled tissue in order to make a tree. As you work up from the bottom, the papers you add should get smaller and smaller.

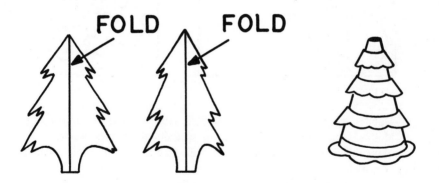

4. CUT PAPER

Different papers are: newspaper, construction paper, wrapping paper, paper bags, cardboard, corrugated paper, tissue paper, cellophane, wallpaper, etc.

Paper can be cut, curled, bent, folded, fringed or scored. You can use any of these to decorate the surface of a piece of paper.

You can freely move your cut pieces on the background until you like the design, then paste the pieces down.

You can make a tree out of cardboard, showing only the trunk and branches. Then attach cut paper leaves. The tree should be supported from the back.

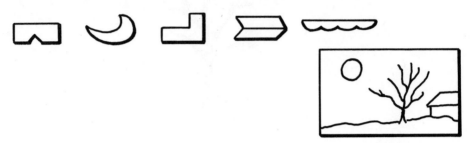

5. COLLAGE

Collage is the putting together of textured and colored papers to make a design. The important thing to remember is the *way* you put the colors, shapes and textured paper together.

A firm paper or cardboard may be used to prevent curling after drying. Cut or tear the paper into shapes. The shapes, color and texture should give you an effect you want. Then move the pieces around until you like the design. Next, paste the shapes.

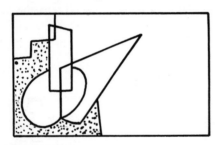
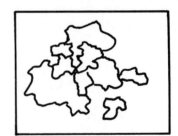

6. MOBILES

Mobiles are moving forms attached by a string to balsa wood, wire or cardboard. Mobile shapes can be made from paper, cardboard or balsa wood.

Move the shapes around until they seem to go together. Then, attach them with string to a stick.

Arrange each stick until the whole mobile is balanced.

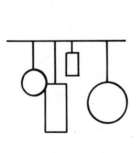
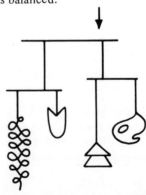

7. CLAY

Clay can be shaped into a form by rolling it, or pulling it. Clay can be pressed or stamped. Clay can be carved.

You can smooth clay with a sponge. You can make designs on your shape by using pencils, combs, sticks or anything you can find.

You can cut a shape from a flat piece of clay. You can cut out the background from a flat piece, making the shape stand out. Small coils or balls of clay can be added when it is wet.

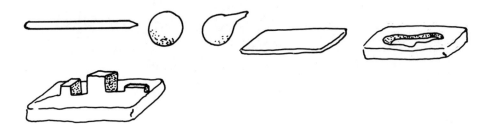

8. STITCHERY

Collect your own materials in a shoe box. Some of the materials you might like to get are: wool, silk and cotton scraps; string, ribbon, buttons, beads or seeds.

You will need to have: large eye needles, scissors, a piece of cloth like burlap from an old potato sack, and wool or cotton yarn in some bright colors.

You can use any stitch you want. If you do not know how to begin, ask your teacher or your mother to show you one simple stitch. Also, look in a stitchery book for simple stitches. Practice those simple stitches on a scrap piece of cloth. Invent your own stiches to fit your idea. Pieces of cloth or seeds, etc., can be stitched on to the stitchery work. Experiment and have fun with stitches!

9. DIORAMA

A diorama has stand-up constructions, placed in a box.

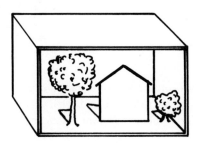

10. PANORAMA

A panorama has stand-up constructions placed on a flat surface, like a table. It shows a scene or tells a story.

These stand-up pieces can be cut out of paper, or made out of many different kinds of materials and placed on the table.

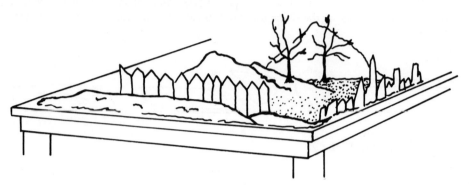

11. PRINTING

POTATO, CARROTS

A potato and/or carrot, spoon, sandpaper, knife or sharp-edged tool will be needed.

Cut the potato or carrot in half (or long way) with a sharp tool.

Draw a design on the cut end. Make sharp cuts. Be careful not to undercut.

The potato will keep 3-4 weeks if covered with waxed paper.

Liquid tempera, water color, or mixture of clay and tempera can be used for paint. Paint may be spread on waxed paper or painted on the surface of the potato with a brush.

For a clear print, put paint on evenly. For a sloppy or careless look, put paint on unevenly. Print on any kind of cloth or paper you wish. Investigate.

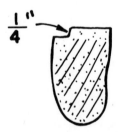

CUT SIDE

RUBBED DESIGNS

Place a sheet of thin colored or white paper over one or more rough objects. Then run the crayon held on its side back and forth over the surface. The raised parts can be seen on the paper. Try rubbing different colors and see what happens.

12. MURAL MAKING

Make large pictures on butcher paper. The pictures can tell a story. Chalk, crayon, brush pen can be used for drawing. Work for large figures. Finish the mural using paint, torn paper, cut-outs, or in any way you wish.

13. POSTERS

Use a simple design, drawing and/or lettering. Make large and small letters that are easily read. Use bright colors. Tempera, crayons, cut-outs are some of the materials that may be used. A heavier paper might be easier to work on. The size is up to you.

 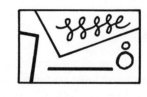

14. MAP MAKING

On an outline map, draw or paste cut-outs of tree forms. Arrange the forms in any way you wish. To make a relief type map, try using a salt and flour mixture or sawdust mache.

15. DESIGN

ABSTRACT (WITH INDIA INK)

You will need tempera, India ink, brush and heavy paper. First, paint a design or picture with tempera. Then add texture in different places. When the tempera dries, fill in white areas with India ink. When ink dries, wash paper lightly. Tempera will wash off. Ink will stay. The design or picture should look like a block print.

16. WALL DISPLAYS

Arrange a collection of pictures, drawings for room or school display. In planning the display, try to break up space into large, simple but interesting areas and shapes. Try using colored paper, yarn, string, etc. to give it that special effect (look).

Lettering should also be planned as part of the whole design.

LESSON II

OBJECTIVE:

After observing a visual of an old apple tree, the student will create something in art.

INSTRUCTIONS:

Choose any one of the items listed under HELPFUL IDEAS, which might help you get a better idea of an old tree.

When you feel you have an idea of how an old tree looks, do any of the activities listed under THINGS TO DO.

See HELPFUL IDEAS and THINGS TO DO, pages 193 and 195.

LESSON III

OBJECTIVE:

After imagining or reviewing an apple tree standing alone, the student will create something in art.

INSTRUCTIONS:

Choose any one of the items listed under HELPFUL IDEAS which might help you to see how a tree looks standing alone.

Once you have the idea, do any one of the activities listed under THINGS TO DO.

See HELPFUL IDEAS and THINGS TO DO, pages 193 and 195.

POST–EVALUATION

When you have completed lessons one, two and three, go to your teacher for your UNIPAC Post-Test.

QUEST OPPORTUNITIES

After you have successfully passed the UNIPAC Post-Test, you might be interested in having some more fun in art. The following quest opportunities are suggested as other areas of self-expression. When you have decided what quest you would like to explore, please discuss it with your teacher.

1. Observing a new cobweb can create a feeling for self-expression.
2. An object thrown into a pool of water creates a feeling for self-expression.
3. Watching smoke rise from a chimney can create a feeling for self-expression.
4. Listening to the sound of wind while in a room creates a different atmosphere for self-expression.
5. Observe a rock with a hole in it.
6. Look at an old bottle found at the beach.

APPENDIX E

Sample Educational Instrument

Individualized Learning Packages (ILP)

in use at

Ruby S. Thomas Elementary School

Las Vegas, Nevada

MAIN IDEA:

Operations on Sets

YOUR OBJECTIVE:

Given a description of the members of two or more sets, you will be able to combine the sets to make a new set called the union set.

PRE-TEST

1. Set A = (cat, dog, cow, horse)
   Set B = (duck, horse, pig)

   Which one of these sets is the union of Set A and Set B?

   Set X = (cat, cow, dog, duck, horse, pig)
   Set Y = (cow, horse, duck, horse, pig)
   Set Z = (cat, dog, cow, hen, duck, horse, pig)

   NOW, complete this statement: $A \cup B =$ _____

2. Set J = (white, blue)
   Set K = (red, blue)   COMPLETE: $J \cup K =$ _____

In items 3-5 find each answer set:

3. $(1,2,3) \cup (5,6) =$
4. $(1,2,3,) \cup (3,4,5) =$
5. $(26,27,28,29) \cup (26,28,30) =$

DIRECTIONS:

Did you miss more than one item on the pre-test: Yes!! Don't weep... Just think of what you *can* learn by doing an activity or two your programmer provided for you in this lesson.

Lucky you—only one miss or was it a perfect hit!!
Try This Then:
How is the union operation related to number operations?
Now: On to lesson 00-Sets-2 or do you have a preference of your own:
If so—confer with your teacher.

Written by: Evelyn Bozarth

Program Directors: Evelyn Bozarth, Andrew Erskine, Gary Fletcher

To order samples or classroom quantities contact the ILP office at Ruby S. Thomas Elementary School, Las Vegas, Nevada

MAIN IDEA:

Operations on Sets

OUR OBJECTIVE:

Given a description of the members of two or more sets, you will be able to combine the sets to make a new set called the union set.
Example: $(a, b, c) \cup (b, c, d) = (a, b, c, d)$

WAYS TO LEARN THIS OBJECTIVE:

1. Find several classmates also working on this lesson to work with you as a team to do the following:
   a. Look in a dictionary for the definition of the word union. Then check items 1-5 on the pre-test and try to determine how the term union is used.
   b. Use a set builder kit. Arrange several sets. Try combining different sets to actually see what is in the union set. Write mathematical sentences for your physical demonstrations.
2. Use Programmed textbook, Spooner, *Mathematics Enrichment, Program B.,* 1962 (The BLUE BOOK)
   a. Answer items 129-224 on pages 29-44. (If you think you have achieved the objective for this lesson before you get to item 224, feel free to stop. BUT try the self-test for this lesson to see if you really have achieved the objective.)
   b. Record your answers on your spelling list tablet. Place tablet over the answers on the right-hand side of each page in the textbook.
   c. Number the items on your tablet to correspond with the numbered items in the textbook. You begin with item #129 on page 29.
   d. Read each each item carefully before recording your answer. When you have answered all items on any page, go back and check your answers with the textbook to see if you understand the material on that page.
   e. If you are satisfied that you do understand the items on page 29, go on to page 30 and so on until you have achieved the objective for this lesson.
3. If you prefer to use a tape recording along with the BLUE BOOK for activity #2, then use Tape Recording #00-Sets-1.
4. Do exercises in Singer Textbook:
   Book 3, pages 7-9
   Book 4, page 4
   Book 5, page 3
   Book 6, page 3

MAIN IDEA:

Operations on Sets

LEARNING MATERIALS:

Textbooks: Spooner, *Mathematical Enrichment,* Program B. (The BLUE BOOK)
                Singer, Books 3,4,5,6
Audio-visual: Set Builder Kit
                Tape Recording#00-Sets-1

SELF-EVALUATION:

Find the union set:

1. (3,4,5) $\cup$ (6,7) = _____
2. (c,d) $\cup$ (c) = _____
3. (x,y,z) $\cup$ ( ) = _____
4. (Joe, Bill) $\cup$ (Bill, Roy) = _____

QUEST:

How did man develop the number concept? _____
Is it related to sets? _____ If so, how? _____

1. (3,4,5,6,7) 2. (c,d) 3. (x,y,z) 4. (Joe, Bill, Roy)

Sample Educational Instrument

Learning Activity Package (LAP)

in use at
Nova School District
Fort Lauderdale, Florida

A

GUIDANCE
LEARNING ACTIVITY PACKAGE

FOR

INTERMEDIATE CHILDREN

Bettie Y. McComb — Guidance Counselor — Nova Elementary

Fort Lauderdale, Florida

IMPLEMENTING THE "FRIENDS" LAP

A Guidance Procedure
by
Bettie McComb—School Counselor
Nova Elementary School

DEFINITION

The Guidance LAP is a series of selected group and individual activities (role playing, group counseling and discussion, appropriate games and creative activities) geared to the interests, abilities and developmental needs of the child, and centered around a given topic.

RATIONALE

The premise from which these LAPs evolved is that a child is more likely to change his behavior if he has an opportunity to individualize his choices, to "try on" new kinds of behavior in situations somewhat structured so that success is rewarding, and failure teaches, but is not devastating.

PLANNING

This particular LAP, "Friends," was written by the counselor to help meet the developmental needs in the area of social interaction for eleven and twelve year olds in Suite "D." With the exception of some special words, the LAP vocabulary is controlled to the third grade reading level. The 125 children in Suite "D" were randomly distributed into nine groups of fifteen children. Each group reports to the guidance room consecutively throughout the year for seven one-hour sessions—usually Monday, Wednesday and Friday.

SESSION STRUCTURE

Each session focuses on a different kind of activity. The children have freedom to move about the room, to get material, to rehearse plays in the corridor or on the patio, to talk, to visit—in short, to interact with each other in a purposeful way. During discussions brief guidelines are suggested to facilitate participation.

INDIVIDUALIZATION

To encourage individualization and creativity the counselor suggests that each child select a special out-of class activity from the list provided in the LAP, that he may adapt any activity to his own needs or interests, or that he may devise his own special project. The only requirement is that the project be relevant to the theme of the LAP.

ROLE OF THE COUNSELOR

The counselor provides a climate in which each child feels relatively safe to make choices, to experiment with different kinds of behavior, to be creative with action and ideas. The counselor acts as a "facilitator," providing materials, facilities and structure which will give the child an opportunity to practice new ways of interacting. The counselor accepts, clarifies and reinforces feelings, values, and attitudes at the appropriate times. Although the overall focus of a session may be on a particular activity, the counselor will find many opportunities for short counseling intervals on a group or one-to-one basis.

EVALUATION

The evaluation of the 'LAP is two-fold. Student evaluation is built into the LAP and consists of student performance of behavioral goals. The counselor's evaluation of the LAP is effected by two sociograms—one taken the first day of the session and one taken the last day. A comparison of these sociograms reveals interesting changes in the distribution of "friends" within the group. The potential for evaluation and diagnosis by use of the sociogram is being further explored.

RATIONALE

We feel good when we act in a friendly way. This package will help us find out many ways of being friendly. Some you may already know but others may be new to you.

After you find out about friendly ways you will have a chance to practice them in a small group. Then you may use them wherever you want to make friends. The more you practice using friendly ways, the more friends you will have.

This package was written to help you have more friends. Now turn to the next page to see how we are going to learn about being friendly.

I have reviewed this package for content in terms of curriculum and appropriateness.

_____

Ruby Huff (Supervisor)

INTRODUCTION

This is a MINI-LAP. (A mini-lap is like a mini-skirt: it is short, but it covers the subject.) This mini-lap is about how to be friendly.

You will be one of a group of 16 Suite D boys and girls who will meet in the Guidance Room three days a week during your "open-lab" time. You will get to know better each person in your group. You will learn about the qualities of friendliness, how people feel when you are unfriendly to them, and some things you can do to be friendly.

There will be some games to play and, if you wish, some stories about friends for you to read. You may even write some stories and have them printed.

BEHAVIORAL OBJECTIVES

When you finish this **MINI-LAP** you should be able to:

(1) Tell three ways you can show friendliness.

(2) Write, in each square containing the name of a member in your group, at least one positive comment about that person.

GROUP ACTIVITIES

First Day—   1. Meet in the Guidance Room with Guidance Counselor.

2. Print your first and last name on a card and pin it onto your shirt or dress.

3. Play "Checkerboard Friends."

Second Day— 4. Finish your "Checkerboard Friends" game.

5. Group Discussion: "What I Like About My Friends." When the discussion is over, jot down some of the things you learned.

Third Day — Drama Day. You will hear a short story. Volunteer to play the part of someone in the story. Be a real actor (or actress)! Try to forget about yourself and try to be the person in the play.

Fourth Day —Choose someone in the group whom you don't know too well. Make a spinner and play a game of "Friendly Maze" with him. If you are the winner, think of something kind to say to the loser. If you are the loser, think of something to say that shows you are trying to be a good sport. Were you a winner?_____ loser?_____ What did you say when the game was over?

_____

Fifth Day — Group Discussion (1) "How do you feel when someone is unfriendly to you?" (2) "What can you do about it?" Write down some things you learned from this discussion.

Sixth Day — Art Day. We will talk about making collages. You will be given a variety of materials from which to choose. Try to make your collage show how you feel about some aspect of friendliness.

Seventh Day—Evaluation:

(1) You will be given a chart which will have on it the names of everyone in your group. You are to see in how many squares you can write a positive comment about that person.

(2) Write three ways which you have learned to show friendliness.

CHECKERBOARD FRIENDS

DIRECTIONS:

Move around the room. Talk to as many boys and girls as you can.

In each square write—

I. 2.	I. 2.	I. 2.	I. 2.
I. 2.	I. 2.	I. 2.	I. 2.
I. 2.	I. 2.	I. 2.	I. 2.
I. 2.	I. 2.	I. 2.	I. 2.
I. 2.	I. 2.	I. 2.	I. 2.

(1) The name of a boy or girl you talked to.
(2) One interesting thing about this person.
There are ___ boys and girls in this group.
Fill in ___ squares.

WHAT WE LIKE ABOUT OUR FRIENDS

In the spaces below write some words that tell what you like about your friend.

My friend is

_____

_____

_____

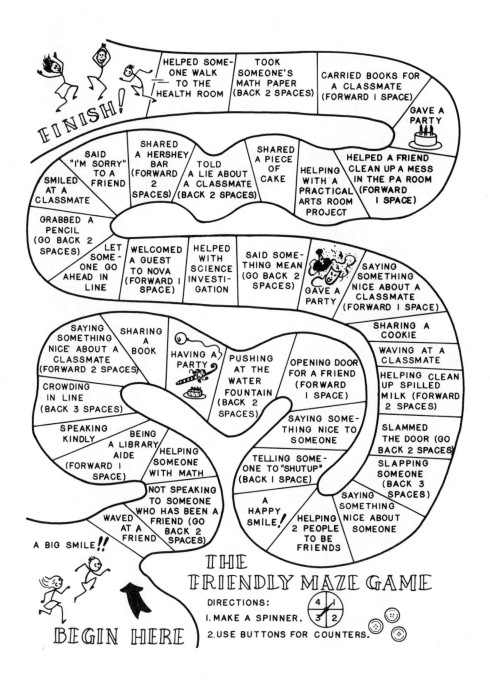

THE FRIENDLY MAZE GAME

DIRECTIONS:
1. MAKE A SPINNER.
2. USE BUTTONS FOR COUNTERS.

BEGIN HERE

_____
_____
_____
_____
_____
_____

SHORT STORIES FOR DRAMA DAY

(Paste your copies of the stories here.)

"FEELINGS"

When someone is unfriendly to me I feel:

(1) _____

(2) _____

(3) _____

Some things I might do when someone is unfriendly to me:

(1) _____

(2) _____

(3) _____

ART DAY

When you have finished your collage, describe it briefly on this page.

SOME SPECIAL ACTIVITIES

Read all of these. Then choose at least one that you would like to do. On the next page in this LAP write a brief description of your special activity.

1. The following books have been especially selected by Mrs. Colden, the Media Specialist, because they tell about friendly people or how to be friendly. Read one or more of the books to find out how people act in a friendly way.

Call Number		Title of Book
394.2	Da	*The Thanksgiving Story*
249	Ma	*Friends with God*
398.2	Bo	*Sam Patch*
363	Ho	*About Friendly Around Town*
E372.2	He	*About School Helpers*
E301.4	Ur	*Big City Neighbors*
B	Sq	*Squanto: Indian Adventurer*
973	Pe	*An American A.B.C.*
331.7	Ho	*About Our Friendly Helpers*
301.3	He	*About More Friendly Helpers*
E323.4	Wi	*Freedom and Our U.S. Family*
395	Ho	*Manners to Grow On*
170	Le	*How to Behave and Why*
821	Mi	*Now We Are Six*
398.2	As	*Told Under the Green Umbrella*
Sc	As	*Told Under the Silver Umbrella*
E		*Two as a Team*
E	Be	*Swimming Hole*
E	Ud	*Let's Be Enemies*
F	Ha	*Two is Company and Three Is a Crowd*
E	Ta	*Almost Big Enough*
E	Da	*Andy and the Lion*
F		*The Big Fish*
362.7	Bu	*Welcome Child*
F	Tw	*Adventures of Huckleberry Finn*
383	Sc	*Adventures of a Letter*
F	Hs	*Adventures of Little Brother*
398.2	Co	*Adventures of Pinocchio*
F	Tr	*The Winter Princess*
E387.7	Br	*I Want to Be an Airline Hostess*
F	Le	*The Rock and the Willows*
F	La	*Jack and Jill*
F	Ca	*Alice Adventures in Wonderland*
E	Al	*Keep your Mouth Closed*
F	Sa	*The Alligators Problem*
F	Ta	*All-of-a-Kind Family*
821.08	Br	*Gaily We Parade*
821.08	Ge	*Family Book of Best Loved Poems*
B	Cl	*America's Mark Twain*
398.2		*Anansi the Spider Man*
F	Kr	*And Now Miguel*
E	An	*Pony for Three*
F	An	*Thumbelina*
E	An	*The Crooked Colt*

E	Bu	*Andrew Henry's Meadow*
F	Ki	*The Jungle Book*
F	Ar	*Diana and Her Rhinoceros*
E	Ar	*Tim's Friend Tower*
E	Mi	*Little Bear's Friend*
F	Be	*Squaw Dog*
F	Si	*Best Friend*
F	Fo	*The Queen Who Flew*
E	Br	*Georgie*

2. Write a short play about friendly people. Perhaps you could put it on during a Drama Day.
3. Go to the P.A. room and make a collage (the word "collage" comes from the French word meaning, "to glue on") of symbols (or signs) of friendliness.
4. View one of the following filmstrips in the Resource Center:

Call Number	Title
177	"New Friends, Good Friends"
177	"Sharing with Others"
175	"Playing Fair"
179	"One Kind of Bravery"

5. Watch people around you at school, at church, at home, at the stores and in your neighborhood. Make a short list of friendly actions you see.

_____
_____
_____
_____

6. In the Resource Center ask at the desk for the following pictures:

Call Number	Title
P-323	News Reporter
Ch-388	Moving Van
Ch-388	Tractor Trailers
Ch-385	Trains
Pi-636	Two Girls
Pi-551.4	Two Children Watering Tulips
Pi-551.4	Two Children with Pump and Pumpkin

(SPECIAL ACTIVITY REPORT SHEET)

My special activity was: _____
_____

Describe your special activity. _____
_____

_____
_____
_____
_____
_____
_____
_____
_____
_____
_____
_____
_____
_____
_____
_____

NAME _____

EVALUATION SHEET

1. In each square write the name of someone in your group. Below each name write, about that person, something which could not be determined just by looking at him. For example: "Jim likes chocolate ice cream." Not: "Jim has blue eyes."

2. Three ways I can show friendliness are:

A. _____

_____

B. _____

_____

C. _____

_____

Announcement

Teacher In-Service Course

on the

Development of Individual Study Units

ANNOUNCEMENT

The Board of Education of Wyandanch
Public Schools, U. F. S. D. 9 hereby
announces the inception of an in-service
course on Monday, May 5, 19__ entitled
THE DEVELOPMENT OF INDIVIDUAL
STUDY UNITS, to be held at the Milton
L. Olive Elementary School, in the Cafe-
torium on Monday and Wednesday of each
week. There will be two (2) courses given.
Section A will be conducted at 3:00 P.M.
and Section B will be conducted at 5:00
P.M. Successful completion of the course
will entitle teachers to three credits toward
a salary increment. The course lectures
will be given by James Lewis, Jr., Chief
School Administrator and other Wyandanch staff members to be designated.

Teacher In-Service
Education Course Title:

THE DEVELOPMENT OF
INDIVIDUAL STUDY UNITS

CONTENT:

>Section I-A
>and
>Section I-B   Introduction

This section will concentrate on familiarizing teachers with the overall format for the development of Individual Study Units. Included will be a comparison of Individual Study Units with Learning Activity Packages of the Nova School in Ft. Lauderdale, Florida; Operation Plan of Hicksville Public Schools, Hicksville, N.Y., and the Contract Method used in Duluth Public Schools, Duluth, Minnesota.

>Section II-A
>and   Rationale
>Section II-B

This section will deal with the function of the Rationale; two different methods for introducing the Rationale and the two ingredients basic to writing a Rationale.

>Section III-A
>and
>Section III-B   Behavioral Objectives

In this section, teachers will be informed of the content of Behavioral Objectives; the three basic ingredients for Behavioral Objectives; the seven thought processes and how they relate to Behavioral Objectives; and the two levels on which Behavioral Objectives may be written.

>Section IV-A
>and
>Section IV-B   Attitudinal Objectives

This section introduces teachers to Attitudinal Objectives; discusses three methods for realizing Attitudinal Objectives; and techniques for distinguishing Attitudinal Objectives from Behavioral Objectives.

>Section V-A
>and   Learning Experience &
>Section V-B   Learning Activity Options

In this section teachers receive insights on how learning experiences may be made relevant to the realities of their students' life experiences; methods which can be used for this purpose; and the various ways in which learning activity options may be introduced which allow for student individuality.

Section VI-A	
and	Pre-Self & Post-Tests
Section VI-B	

This section is designed to acquaint the teacher with methods of writing tests which evaluate the thought processes as they relate to the Behavioral Objectives of the lesson.

Section VII-A	
and	Evaluation
Section VII-B	

This section is designed to inform the teacher of the importance of evaluation and how critical it is in judging the effectiveness of the entire unit.

GENERAL INFORMATION:

All teachers enrolled in the course will receive an Individual Study Unit dealing with each component of Individual Study Units.

Lectures approximately 10 to 15 minutes in length will be conducted by the Chief School Administrator and other staff members to be designated.

Each week, on Tuesdays and Thursdays, in the Board Room of the Straight Path School, the Chief School Administrator will be available for small group, individual and independent work with teachers desiring his assistance. These meetings will be predicated entirely upon the desire of the teacher for individual assistance.

All teachers who wish to participate throughout the summer in the development of Individual Study Units are required to take this course. Those teachers so employed during the summer months will, from time to time during the school year, continue to develop Individual Study Units. Remuneration for these services will be made on a contractual basis, relative to the difficulty of the unit completed, and fees will vary from $30.00 to $50.00 per unit. Projections indicate that teachers should be able to complete between six and ten units per week. Upon completion of an Individual Study Unit, before remuneration will be forthcoming, the unit will be submitted to scrutiny by a survey team to determine its accuracy, appropriateness and relevancy. Payment will be forthcoming upon approval by the survey team.

Memorandum on the
Employment of Teachers

for the
Development of Individual Study Units

WYANDANCH PUBLIC SCHOOLS
Wyandanch, New York

Memo to: All Professional Staff
From: James Lewis, Jr.
              District Principal
Subject: Availability of Summer Curriculum Positions

During this coming summer the Wyandanch School District will employ teachers to write Individual Study Units in the combined area of Language Arts and Social Studies. Teachers writing IS Units will have an option of working in the school district for a period of six weeks at $100 per week or working independently, wages to be based according to the number of units produced.

A total of fifteen teachers will be hired to work in the district. These teachers will work in the air conditioned Resource Center at the Milton L. Olive School. The work period will begin on June 30th and end on August 8th. The working hours will be from 8:30 a.m. to 12:30 p.m. each day.

Compensation above the $600 can be earned by completing a quota of work set by the Director.

Teachers wishing to apply for the in-district positions should complete the attached application forms and give the forms to their building principal no later than Thursday, June 19th at 3:00 p.m. Teachers will be selected based on the recommendation of the Building Principal, the Curriculum Associate and the Project Director. The completion of the IS Unit course is *NOT* a pre-requisite for in-district work.

We want and need good teachers for this project. If you are interested, please complete the application immediately!

Contractual Agreement for Teachers

Working on
Individual Study Units

WYANDANCH PUBLIC SCHOOLS
Wyandanch, New York

CONTRACTUAL AGREEMENT

Terms of Employment — Curriculum Work

The person listed below will be employed by the Wyandanch Public Schools, U.F.S.D.#9. This employment will be for curriculum work indicated below.

NAME   # State Project   # Local Project

No.   Street   Retirement #   Rate of Retirement
                                   (State Teachers or State Employees)

Town   State

                                   Social Security #

CURRICULUM PROJECT

Rate of Pay $_____   per hour

                     $_____   per week

                     $_____   per month

                     $_____   flat rate for project

(Payroll will be on a bi-weekly basis)

Signature of Chairman of Staff   Signature of Employee

Signature of Director of Curriculum

Original and three copies of this form must be filled out for each project employee.

Index

A

Academic achievement test, use of as Placement Test, 80-81

Acquisition of knowledge, attitude towards, 114

Action, acquiring knowledge through, 97-101

Administration of Individualized Instruction Program, containing, 127-139

  classroom, organization of, 127-132

    cluster, 130-132

    self-contained, 127-130

  grouping procedures, 137-139

  procedures for, 132-137

Affective domain, evaluation of, 120-121

Agenda for meeting, preparing as learning experience, 101

American Book Company, 58

Analysis as thought process, 71-72

"Answers and Questions," 33

Application as thought process, 71

Art gallery, visit to as learning experience, 104-105

Articles, writing as learning experience, 101

Asking questions as technique for evaluating attitudes, 121

Attitudinal objective, developing format for, 45-46

Attitudinal objectives, developing, 108-116

  classification of, 114-115

    towards acquisition of knowledge, 114

    towards one's reason, 114

    towards one's self and being, 115

    towards others and their culture, 114-115

    towards world, 115

  components of, 109

  favorable influence on learning, effort to make, 108-109

  levels, five, of attitudinal attainment, 110-112

    believing, 111

    characterization, 111-112

    organization, 111

    receiving, 110-111

    responding, 111

  methods for realizing, 112-114

    examination-question plan, 112

    goals and objectives plan, 112

    learning experience plan, 112-114

  sources of, 109-110

    "correct," 109-110

Attitudinal responses, evaluating, 123-125

Audio-visual aids, using, in development of Individual Study Units, 36

Auto-Tutor, 106

B

Behavioral objectives, defining, 69-79

  evaluating, 121-123

  learning, three types of, 70

  learning as change in, 75

    terms, identifiable, for learning, 76

  thought derivatives, 72-75

    and thought processes, interaction between, 73

  thought processes, seven, 70-72

    analysis, 71-72

    application, 71

    evaluation, 72

    interpretation, 71

    remembering, 70-71

    synthesis, 72

    translating, 71

  writing, two methods for, 75-77

    caution, 78

    Multiple Level Approach, 77

    Single Level Approach, 77

Behavioral objectives of Individual Study

U